RAFA

RAFA

RAFAEL NADAL

and John Carlin

HYPERION

New York

Library of Congress Cataloging-in-Publication Data

Nadal, Rafael.
Rafa / by Rafael Nadal and John Carlin
p. cm.
ISBN 978-1-4013-2451-3 (hardback)
1. Nadal, Rafael.   2. Tennis players—Spain—Biography.
I. Carlin, John.   II. Title.
GV994.N33A3 2011
796.342092—dc23
[B]
2011020769

Hyperion books are available for special promotions and premiums. For details contact the HarperCollins Special Markets Department in the New York office at 212-207-7528, fax 212-207-7222, or email spsales@harpercollins.com.

Book design by Chris Welch

FIRST EDITION

10   9   8   7   6   5   4   3   2   1

CONTENTS

CONTENTS

ACKNOWLEDGMENTS

First, I'd like to thank John Carlin, who made the experience of working on this book a pleasure and an honor. Writing a book with a journalist and author of John's caliber was in itself a great experience. But getting to know John as we worked together and traveled to tournaments in Doha and Australia ensured we became not only collaborators on a project, but friends as well.

Of course, this book would not have been possible without the support of many people. All my love and gratitude to my parents, my sister, my grandparents, my uncles and aunt, and to María Francisca. A big thanks also to my team and close friends: Carlos, Titín, Joan Forcades, Benito, Tuts, Francis, Ángel Ruiz Cotorro, Carlos Moyá, Toméu Salva, M. A. Munar.

And a very special thank you to my uncle, coach, and friend, Toni Nadal.

—RAFAEL NADAL

First I must thank Luis Viñuales, the great coordinator, whose brainchild this book is, as well as Larry Kirshbaum, who got the ball rolling. Also much thanks to my editor at Hyperion, Jill Schwartzman, who has displayed admirable patience and fortitude.

Special thanks to my agent, who is much more than an agent, Anne Edelstein; and to her assistant—far more than the title suggests—Krista Ingebretson. And a big thanks to Arantxa Martinez, whose hard toil and advice and good humor have helped a lot.

Otherwise, it has been an enormous pleasure to work on this book with Rafa Nadal, his family, his team, and his friends, every one of whom has been helpful, considerate, and kind.

—JOHN CARLIN

CAST OF CHARACTERS

The Family

Rafael Nadal: tennis player

Sebastián Nadal: his father
Ana María Parera: his mother
Maribel Nadal: his sister
Toni Nadal: his uncle and coach
Rafael Nadal: his uncle
Miguel Ángel Nadal: his uncle, and former professional
  football player
Marilén Nadal: his aunt and godmother
Don Rafael Nadal: his paternal grandfather
Pedro Parera: his maternal grandfather
Juan Parera: his uncle and godfather

The Team

Carlos Costa: his agent

Rafael Maymó ("Titín"): his physical therapist

Benito Pérez Barbadillo: his communications chief

Joan Forcades: his physical trainer

Francis Roig: his second coach

Jordi Robert ("Tuts"): his Nike handler and close friend

Ángel Ruiz Cotorro: his doctor

Jofre Porta: a coach when he was young

The Friends

María Francisca Perelló: his girlfried

Carlos Moyá: former world number one tennis player

Toméu Salva: childhood tennis-playing friend

Miguel Ángel Munar: his oldest friend

RAFA

CHAPTER 1

THE SILENCE OF THE CENTRE COURT

HE SILENCE, THAT'S what strikes you when you play on Wimbledon's Centre Court. You bounce the ball soundlessly up and down on the soft turf; you toss it up to serve; you hit it and you hear the echo of your own shot. And of every shot after that. *Clack, clack; clack, clack.* The trimmed grass, the rich history, the ancient stadium, the players dressed in white, the respectful crowds, the venerable tradition—not a billboard advertisement in view—all combine to enclose and cushion you from the outside world. The feeling suits me; the cathedral hush of the Centre Court is good for my game. Because what I battle hardest to do in a tennis match is to quiet the voices in my head, to shut everything out of my mind but the contest itself and concentrate every atom of my being on the point I am playing. If I made a mistake on a previous point, forget it; should a thought of victory suggest itself, crush it.

The silence of the Centre Court is broken when a point's done, if it's been a good point—because the Wimbledon crowds can tell the difference—by a shock of noise; applause, cheers, people shouting your name. I hear them, but as if from some place far off. I don't register that there are fifteen thousand people hunched around the arena, tracking every move my opponent and I make. I am so focused I have no sense at all, as I do now reflecting back on the Wimbledon final of 2008 against Roger Federer, the biggest match of my life, that there are millions watching me around the world.

I had always dreamt of playing here at Wimbledon. My uncle Toni, who has been my coach all my life, had drummed into me from an early age that this was the biggest tournament of them all. By the time I was fourteen, I was sharing with my friends the fantasy that I'd play here one day and win. So far, though, I'd played and lost, both times against Federer—in the final here the year before, and the year before that. The defeat in 2006 had not been so hard. I went out onto the court that time just pleased and grateful that, having just turned twenty, I'd made it that far. Federer beat me pretty easily, more easily than if I'd gone out with more belief. But my defeat in 2007, which went to five sets, left me utterly destroyed. I knew I could have done better, that it was not my ability or the quality of my game that had failed me, but my head. And I wept after that loss. I cried incessantly for half an hour in the dressing room. Tears of disappointment and self-recrimination. Losing always hurts, but it hurts much more when you had your chance and threw it away. I had beaten myself as much as Federer had beaten me; I had let myself down and I hated that. I had flagged mentally, I had allowed myself to get distracted; I had veered from my game plan. So stupid, so unnecessary. So obviously, so exactly what you must not do in a big game.

My uncle Toni, the toughest of tennis coaches, is usually the last person in the world to offer me consolation; he criticizes me even when I win. It is a measure of what a wreck I must have been that he abandoned the habit of a lifetime and told me there was no reason to cry, that there would be more Wimbledons and more Wimbledon finals. I told him he didn't understand, that this had probably been my last time here, my last chance to win it. I am very, very keenly aware of how short the life of a professional athlete is, and I cannot bear the thought of squandering an opportunity that might never come again. I know I won't be happy when my career is over, and I want to make the best of it while it lasts. Every single moment counts—that's why I've always trained very hard— but some moments count for more than others, and I had let a big one pass in 2007. I'd missed an opportunity that might never come again; just two or three points here or there, had I been more focused, would have made all the difference. Because victory in tennis turns on the tiniest of margins. I'd lost the last and fifth set 6–2 against Federer, but had I just been a little more clearheaded when I was 4–2 or even 5–2 down, had I seized my four chances to break his serve early on in the set (instead of seizing up, as I did), or had I played as if this were the first set and not the last, I could have won it.

There was nothing Toni could do to ease my grief. Yet he turned out, in the end, to be right. Another chance had come my way. Here I was again, just one year later. I was determined now that I'd learn the lesson from that defeat twelve months earlier, that whatever else gave way this time, my head would not. The best sign that my head was in the right place now was the conviction, for all the nerves, that I would win.

At dinner with family and friends and team members the night before, at the house we rent when I play at Wimbledon, across the road from the All England Club, mention of the match had been off-limits. I didn't expressly prohibit them from raising the subject, but they all understood well enough that, whatever else I might have been talking about, I was already beginning to play the match in a space inside my head that, from here on in until the start of play, should remain mine alone. I cooked, as I do most nights during the Wimbledon fortnight. I enjoy it, and my family thinks it's good for me. Something else to help settle my mind. That night I grilled some fish and served some pasta with shrimps. After dinner I played darts with my uncles Toni and Rafael, as if this were just another evening at home in Manacor, the town on the Spanish island of Mallorca where I have always lived. I won. Rafael claimed later that he'd let me win, so I'd be in a better frame of mind for the final, but I don't believe him. It's important for me to win, at everything. I have no sense of humor about losing.

At a quarter to one I went to bed, but I couldn't sleep. The subject we had chosen not to talk about was the only one on my mind. I watched films on TV and only dozed off at four in the morning. At nine I was up. It would have been better to have slept a few hours more, but I felt fresh, and Rafael Maymó, my physical therapist, who is always in attendance, said it made no difference—that the excitement and the adrenaline would carry me through, however long the game went on.

For breakfast I had my usual. Some cereal, orange juice, a milk chocolate drink—never coffee—and my favorite from home, bread sprinkled with salt and olive oil. I'd woken up feeling good. Tennis is so much about how you feel on the day. When you get up in the morning, any ordinary morning, sometimes you feel bright and healthy and strong; other days you feel muggy and fragile. That day I felt as alert and nimble and full of energy as I ever had.

It was in that mood that at ten thirty I crossed the road for my final training session at Wimbledon's Court 17, close to the Centre Court. Before I started hitting, I lay down on a bench, as I always do, and Rafael Maymó—who I nickname "Titín"—bent and stretched my knees, massaged my legs, my shoulder, and then gave special attention to my feet. (My left foot is the most vulnerable part of my body, where it hurts most often, most painfully.) The idea is to wake up the muscles and reduce the possibility of injuries. Usually I'd hit balls for an hour in the warm-up before a big match, but this time, because it was drizzling, I left it after twenty-five minutes. I started gently, as always, and gradually increased the pace until I ended up running and hitting with the same intensity as in a match. I trained with more nerves than usual that morning, but also with greater concentration. Toni was there and so was Titín, and my agent, Carlos Costa, a former professional tennis player, who was there to warm up with me. I was more quiet than usual. We all were. No jokes. No smiles. When we wrapped up, I could tell, just from a glance, that Toni was not too happy, that he felt I hadn't been hitting the ball as cleanly as I might have. He looked reproachful—I've known that look all my life—and worried. He was right that I hadn't been at my sharpest just then, but I knew something that he didn't, and never could, enormously important as he had been in the whole of my tennis career: physically I felt in perfect shape, save for a pain on the sole of my left foot that I'd have to have treated before I went on court, and inside I bore the single-minded conviction that I had it in me to win. Tennis against a rival with whom you're evenly matched, or whom you have a chance of beating, is all about raising your game when it's needed. A champion plays at his best not in the opening rounds of a tournament but in the semi-finals and finals against the best opponents, and a great tennis champion plays at his best in a Grand Slam final. I had my fears—I was in a constant battle to contain my nerves—but I fought them down, and the one thought that occupied my brain was that today I'd rise to the occasion.

I was physically fit and in good form. I had played very well a month earlier at the French Open, where I'd beaten Federer in the final, and I'd played some incredible games here on grass. The two last times we'd met here at Wimbledon he'd gone in as the favorite. This year I still felt I wasn't the favorite. But there was a difference. I didn't think that Federer was the favorite to win either. I put my chances at fifty-fifty.

I also knew that, most probably, the balance of poorly chosen or poorly struck shots would stand at close to fifty-fifty between us by the time it was all over. That is in the nature of tennis, especially with two players as familiar with each other's game as Federer and I are. You might think that after the millions and millions of balls I've hit, I'd have the basic shots of tennis sown up, that reliably hitting a true, smooth, clean shot every time would be a piece of cake. But it isn't. Not just because every day you wake up feeling differently, but because every shot is different; every single one. From the moment the ball is in motion, it comes at you at an infinitesimal number of angles and speeds; with more topspin, or backspin, or flatter, or higher. The differences might be minute, microscopic, but so are the variations your body makes—shoulders, elbow, wrists, hips, ankles, knees—in every shot. And there are so many other factors—the weather, the surface, the rival. No ball arrives the same as another; no shot is identical. So every time you line up to hit a shot, you have to make a split-second judgment as to the trajectory and speed of the ball and then make a split-second decision as to how, how hard, and where you must try and hit the shot back. And you have to do that over and over, often fifty times in a game, fifteen times in twenty seconds, in continual bursts more than two, three, four hours, and all the time you're running hard and your nerves are taut; it's when your coordination is right and the tempo is smooth that the good sensations come, that you are better able to manage the biological and mental feat of striking the ball cleanly in the middle of the racket and aiming it true, at speed and under immense mental pressure, time after time. And of one thing I have no doubt: the more you train, the better your feeling. Tennis is, more than most sports, a sport of the mind; it is the player who has those good sensations on the most days, who manages to isolate himself best from his fears and from the ups and downs in morale a match inevitably brings, who ends up being world number one. This was the goal I had set myself during my four patient years as number two to Federer, and which I knew I would be very close to reaching if I won this Wimbledon final.

When the match itself would actually begin was another question. I looked up and saw patches of blue in the sky. But it was mostly overcast, with thick, dark clouds glowering on the horizon. The game was due to start in three hours, but there was every chance it might be delayed or interrupted. I didn't let that worry me. My mind was going to be clear and focused this time, whatever happened. No distractions. I was not going to allow any room for a repeat of my failure of concentration in 2007.

We left Court 17 at about eleven-thirty and went to the locker room, the one at the All England Club that's reserved for the top seeds. It's not very big, maybe a quarter of the size of a tennis court. But the tradition of the place is what gives it its grandeur. The wood panels, the green and purple colors of Wimbledon on the walls, the carpeted floor, the knowledge that so many greats—Laver, Borg, McEnroe, Connors, Sampras—have been there. Usually it's busy in there, but now that there were just the two of us left in the tournament, I was alone. Federer hadn't showed up yet. I had a shower, changed, and went up a couple of flights of stairs to have lunch in the players' dining room. Again, it was unusually quiet, but this suited me. I was withdrawing deeper into myself, isolating myself from my surroundings, settling into the routines—the inflexible routines— I have before each match and that continue right up to the start of play. I ate what I always eat. Pasta—no sauce, nothing that could possibly cause indigestion—with olive oil and salt, and a straight, simple piece of fish. To drink: water. Toni and Titín were at the table with me. Toni was brooding. But that's nothing new. Titín was placid. He is the person in whose company I spend the most time and he's always placid. Again, we spoke little. I think Toni might have grumbled about the weather, but I said nothing. Even when I'm not playing a tournament, I listen more than I talk.

At one o'clock, with an hour to go before the start of play, we went back down to the locker room. An unusual thing about tennis is that even in the biggest tournaments you share a locker room with your opponent. Federer was already in there, sitting on the wooden bench where he always sits, when I came in after lunch. Because we're used to it, there was no awkwardness. None that I felt, anyway. In a little while we were going to do everything we possibly could to crush each other in the biggest match of the year, but we're friends as well as rivals. Other rivals in sports might hate each other's guts even when they're not playing against each other. We don't. We like each other. When the game starts, or is about to start, we put the friendship to one side. It's nothing personal. I do it with everybody around me, even my family. I stop being the ordinary me when a game is on. I try and become a tennis machine, even if the task is ultimately impossible. I am not a robot; perfection in tennis is impossible, and trying to scale the peak of your possibilities is where the challenge lies. During a match you are in a permanent battle to fight back your everyday vulnerabilities, bottle up your human feelings. The more bottled up they are, the greater your chances of winning, so long as you've trained as hard as you play and the gap in talent is not too wide between you and your rival. The gap in talent with Federer existed, but it was not impossibly wide. It was narrow enough, even on his favorite surface in the tournament he played best, for me to know that if I silenced the doubts and fears, and exaggerated hopes, inside my head better than he did, I could beat him. You have to cage yourself in protective armor, turn yourself into a bloodless warrior. It's a kind of self-hypnosis, a game you play, with deadly seriousness, to disguise your own weaknesses from yourself, as well as from your rival.

To joke or chatter about football with Federer in the locker room, as we might before an exhibition match, would have been a lie he would have seen through immediately and interpreted as a sign of fear. Instead, we did each other the courtesy of being honest. We shook hands, nodded, exchanged the faintest of smiles, and stepped over to our respective lockers, maybe ten paces away from each other, and then each pretended the other wasn't there. Not that I really needed to pretend. I was in that locker room and I wasn't. I was retreating into some place deep inside my head, my movements increasingly programmed, automatic.

Forty-five minutes before the game was scheduled to start I took a cold shower. Freezing cold water. I do this before every match. It's the point before the point of no return; the first step in the last phase of what I call my pre-game ritual. Under the cold shower I enter a new space in which I feel my power and resilience grow. I'm a different man when I emerge. I'm activated. I'm in "the flow," as sports psychologists describe a state of alert concentration in which the body moves by pure instinct, like a fish in a current. Nothing else exists but the battle ahead.

Just as well, because the next thing I had to do was not something that, in ordinary circumstances, I would accept with calm. I went downstairs to a small medical room to have my doctor give me a painkilling injection in the sole of my left foot. I'd had a blister and a swelling around one of the tiny metatarsal bones down there since the third round. That part of the foot had to be put to sleep, otherwise I simply couldn't have played—the pain would have been too great.

Then it was up to the locker room again and back to my ritual. I put on my earphones and listened to music. It sharpens that sense of flow, removes me further from my surroundings. Then Titín bandaged my left foot. While he did that, I put the grips on my rackets, all six I'd be taking on court. I always do this. They come with a black pre-grip. I roll a white tape over the black one, spinning the tape around and around, working diagonally up the shaft. I don't need to think about it, I just do it. As if in a trance.

Next I lay down on a massage table and Titín wrapped a couple of straps of bandage around my legs, just below the knees. I'd had aches there too, and the straps helped prevent soreness, or eased the pain if it came.

Playing sports is a good thing for ordinary people; sport played at the professional level is not good for your health. It pushes your body to limits that human beings are not naturally equipped to handle. That's why just about every top professional athlete has been laid low by injury, sometimes a career-ending injury. There was a moment in my career when I seriously wondered whether I'd be able to continue competing at the top level. I play through pain much of the time, but I think all elite sports people do. All except Federer, at any rate. I've had to push and mold my body to adapt it to cope with the repetitive muscular stress that tennis forces on you, but he just seems to have been born to play the game. His physique—his DNA—seems perfectly adapted to tennis, rendering him immune to the injuries the rest of us are doomed to put up with. They tell me he doesn't train as hard as I do. I don't know if it's true, but it would figure. You get these blessed freaks of nature in other sports too. The rest of us just have to learn to live with pain, and long breaks from the game, because a foot, a shoulder, or a leg has sent a cry for help to the brain, asking it to stop. That's why I need to have so much bandaging done before a match; that's why it's such a critical part of my preparations.

After Titín had done my knees, I stood up, got dressed, went to a basin, and ran water through my hair. Then I put on my bandanna. It's another maneuver that requires no thought, but I do it slowly, carefully, tying it tightly and very deliberately behind the back of my head. There's a practical point to it: keeping my hair from falling over my eyes. But it's also another moment in the ritual, another decisive moment of no return, like the cold shower, when my sense is sharpened that very soon I'll be entering battle.

It was nearly time to go on court. The adrenaline rush, creeping up on me all day, flooded my nervous system. I was breathing hard, bursting to release energy. But I had to sit still a moment longer as Titín bandaged the fingers of my left hand, my playing hand, his moves as mechanical and silent as mine when I wrap the grips around my rackets. There's nothing cosmetic about this. Without the bandages, the skin would stretch and tear during the game.

I stood up and began exercising, violently—activating my explosiveness, as Titín calls it. Toni was on hand, watching me, not saying much. I didn't know whether Federer was watching me too. I just know he's not as busy as I am in the locker room before a match. I jumped up and down, ran in short bursts from one end of the cramped space to the other—no more than six meters or so. I stopped short, rotated my neck, my shoulders, my wrists, crouched down and bent my knees. Then more jumps, more mini sprints, as if I were alone in my gym back home. Always with my earphones on, the music pumping inside my head. I went to take a pee. (I find myself taking a lot of pees—nervous pees—just before a game, sometimes five or six in that final hour.) Then I came back, swung my arms high and round my shoulders, hard.

Toni gestured, I took off the earphones. He said there was a rain delay, but for no more than fifteen minutes, they thought. I wasn't fazed. I was ready for this. Rain would have the same effect on Federer as it would on me. No need to be thrown off balance. I sat down and checked my rackets, felt the balance, the weight; pulled up my socks, checked that both were exactly the same height on my calves. Toni leaned close to me. "Don't lose sight of the game plan. Do what you have to do." I was listening but I was not listening. I know at these moments what I have to do. I think my concentration is good. My endurance too. Endurance: that's a big word. Keeping going physically, never letting up, and putting up with everything that comes my way, not allowing the good or the bad—the great shots or the weak ones, the good luck or the bad—to put me off track. I have to be centered, no distractions, do what I have to do in each moment. If I have to hit the ball twenty times to Federer's backhand, I'll hit it twenty times, not nineteen. If I have to wait for the rally to stretch to ten shots or twelve or fifteen to bide my chance to hit a winner, I'll wait. There are moments when you have a chance to go for a winning drive, but you have a 70 percent chance of succeeding; you wait five shots more and your odds will have improved to 85 percent. So be alert, be patient, don't be rash.

If I go up to the net, I hit it to his backhand, not to his drive, his strongest shot. Losing your concentration means going to the net and hitting the ball to his forehand, or omitting in a rush of blood to serve to his backhand—always to his backhand—or going for a winner when it's not time. Being concentrated means keeping doing what you know you have to do, never changing your plan, unless the circumstances of a rally or of the game change exceptionally enough to warrant springing a surprise. It means discipline, it means holding back when the temptation arises to go for broke. Fighting that temptation means keeping your impatience or frustration in check.

Even if you see what seems like a chance to put the pressure on and seize the initiative, keep hitting to the backhand, because in the long run, over the course of the whole game, that is what's wisest and best. That's the plan. It's not a complicated plan. You can't even call it a tactic, it's so simple. I play the shot that's easier for me and he plays the one that's harder for him—I mean, my left-handed drive against his right-handed backhand. It's just a question of sticking to it. With Federer what you have to do is keep applying pressure to the backhand, make him play the ball high, strike with the racket up where his neck is, put him under pressure, wear him down. Probe chinks that way in his game and his morale. Frustrate him, drive him close to despair, if you can. And when he is striking the ball well, as he most surely will, for you won't have him in trouble the whole time, not by any means, chase down every attempted winner of his, hit it back deep, make him feel he has to win the point two, three, four times to get to 15–love.

That's all I was thinking, in so far as you can say I was thinking at all, as I sat there fiddling with my rackets and socks and the bandages on my fingers, music filling my head, waiting for the rain to pass. Until an official with a blazer walked in and told us it was time. I sprang up, swung my shoulders, rolled my neck from side to side, did a couple more bursts up and down the locker room.

Now I was supposed to hand over my bag to a court attendant

for him to carry it to my chair. It's part of Wimbledon protocol on Final Day. It doesn't happen anywhere else. I don't like it. It's a break from my routine. I handed over my bag but took out one racket. I led the way out of the locker room clutching the racket hard, along corridors with photographs of past champions and trophies behind glass frames, down some stairs and left and out into the cool English July air and the magical green of the Centre Court.

I sat down, took off my white track suit top, and took a sip from a bottle of water. Then from a second bottle. I repeat the sequence, every time, before a match begins, and at every break between games, until a match is over. A sip from one bottle, and then from another. And then I put the two bottles down at my feet, in front of my chair to my left, one neatly behind the other, diagonally aimed at the court. Some call it superstition, but it's not. If it were superstition, why would I keep doing the same thing over and over whether I win or lose? It's a way of placing myself in a match, ordering my surroundings to match the order I seek in my head.

Federer and the umpire were standing at the foot of the umpire's chair, waiting for the coin toss. I leapt up, stood across the net from Federer, and began to run in place, to jump energetically up and down. Federer stood still, always so much more relaxed than me, in appearance anyway.

The last part of ritual, as important as all the preparations that went before, was to look up, scan the perimeter of the stadium, and search for my family members among the blur of the Centre Court crowd, locking their exact coordinates inside my head. At the other end of the court to my left, are my father and mother and my uncle Toni; and diagonally across from them, behind my right shoulder, my sister, three of my grandparents and my godfather and godmother, who are also my uncle and aunt, plus another uncle. I don't let them intrude on my thoughts during a match—I don't ever let myself smile during a match—but knowing they are there, as they always have been, gives me the peace of mind on which my success as a player rests. I build a wall around myself when I play, but my family is the cement that holds the wall together.

I also looked in the crowd for the members of my team, the professionals I employ. Sitting alongside my parents and Toni, Carlos Costa, my agent and great friend, was there; and Benito Pérez Barbadillo, my press chief; and Jordi Robert—I call him "Tuts"—who is my handler at Nike; and Titín, who knows me most intimately of all and is like a brother to me. I could also see, in my mind's eye, my paternal grandfather and my girfriend, María Francisca, whom I call Mary, watching me on television back home in Manacor, and the two other members of my team who were also absent, but not for that any less critical to my success: Francis Roig, my second coach, as clever a tennis man as Toni, but more easygoing, and my smart, intense physical trainer Joan Forcades who, like Titín, ministers as much to my mind as he does to my body.

My immediate family, my extended family, and my professional team (all of whom are practically family themselves) stand in three concentric rings around me. Not only do they cocoon me from the dangerously distracting hurly-burly that comes with money and fame, together they create the environment of affection and trust I need to allow my talent to flower. Each individual member of the group complements the other; each plays his or her role in fortifying me where I am weak, boosting me where I am strong. To imagine my good fortune and success in their absence is to imagine the impossible.

Roger won the toss. He chose to serve. I didn't mind. I like my rival to start serving at the beginning of a match. If my head is strong, if his nerves are getting to him, I know I have a good chance of breaking him. I thrive on the pressure. I don't buckle; I grow stronger on it. The closer to the precipice I am, the more elated I feel. Of course I feel nerves, and of course the adrenaline and the blood are pumping so hard I can feel them from my temples to my legs. It's an extreme state of physical alertness, but conquerable. I did conquer it. The adrenaline beat the nerves. My legs didn't give way. They felt strong, ready to run all day. I was bristling. I was locked away in my solitary tennis world but I'd never felt more alive.

We took our positions on the baselines and started warming up. That echoing silence again: *clack, clack; clack, clack.* Somewhere in my mind I took note, not for the first time, of just how fluent and easy Roger was in his movements; how poised. I'm more of a scrapper. More defensive, scrambling, recovering, on the brink. I know that's my image; I've watched myself often enough on videos. And it's a fair reflection of how I've played most of my career—especially when Federer has been my rival. But the good sensations remained. My preparations had worked well. The emotions that would assail and overwhelm me if I hadn't performed my ritual, if I hadn't systematically willed myself into shedding the stage fright the Centre Court would ordinarily induce, were under control, if not altogether gone. The wall I'd built around myself stood solid and tall. I'd achieved the right balance between tension and control, between nerves and the conviction I could win. And I was striking the ball hard and true: the ground strokes, the volleys, the smashes, and then the serves with which we wrapped up the sparring session before the real battle began. I went back to my chair, toweled my arms, my face, sipped from each of my two bottles of water. I had a flashback to this stage in last year's final, just before play started. I said to myself one more time that I was ready to accept whatever problems

came my way and that I would overcome them. Because winning
this match was the dream of my life and I'd never been closer to
reaching it and I might not have another chance again. Something
else might fail me, my knee or my foot, my backhand or my serve,
but my head would not. I might feel fear, the nerves might get the
better of me at some point, but over the long haul my head, this
time, was not going to let me down.

"CLARK KENT AND SUPERMAN"

THE RAFA NADAL the world saw as he stormed onto the Centre Court lawn for the start of the 2008 Wimbledon final was a warrior, eyes glazed in murderous concentration, clutching his racket like a Viking clutches his axe. A glance at Federer revealed a striking contrast in styles: the younger player in sleeveless shirt and pirate's pantaloons, the older one in a cream, gold-embossed cardigan and classic Fred Perry shirt; one playing the part of the street-fighting underdog, the other suave and effortlessly superior.

If Nadal, veined biceps bulging, was a picture of elemental brute force, Federer—lean and lithe, five years older at twenty-seven—was all natural grace. If Nadal, who had just turned twenty-two, was the head-down assassin, Federer was the aristocrat who strolled on court waving airily to the multitudes as if he owned Wimbledon, as if he were welcoming guests to a private garden party.

Federer's absent-minded, almost supercilious demeanor during the pre-match warm-up hardly hinted at the game's billing as a clash of titans; Nadal's thunderous intensity was a grunting caricature of a PlayStation action hero. Nadal hits his forehands as if he were firing a rifle. He cocks an imaginary gun, eyes the target, and pulls the trigger. With Federer—whose name means "trader in feathers" in old German—there is no sense of pause, no visible mechanism. He is all unforced liquidity. Nadal (the name means "Christmas" in Catalan or Mallorcan, a word with altogether more exuberant associations than "feather trader"), was the super fit, self-built sportsman of the modern era; Federer belonged to a type one might have seen in the 1920s, when tennis was an upper-crust pastime, a gentlemen's spirited exercise following afternoon tea.

That was what the world saw. What Federer saw was a snarling young pretender who threatened to usurp his tennis kingdom, stop his quest for a record of six consecutive Wimbledon victories, and displace him from the position he had held for four years as world number one. The effect Nadal had on Federer in the locker room before the match began had to be intimidating, otherwise, in the view of Francis Roig, Nadal's second coach, "Federer would have had to be made of stone."

"It's the moment he gets up from the massage table, after Maymó has finished putting on his bandages, that he becomes scary for his rivals," says Roig, himself a former tennis professional. "The simple action of wrapping on his bandanna is so frighteningly intense; his eyes, far away, seem to see nothing that's around him. Then, suddenly, he'll breathe deep and kick into life, pumping his legs up and down and then, as if oblivious to the fact that his rival is just a few paces away across the room, he'll let out a cry of 'Vamos! Vamos!' ['Let's go! Let's go!']. There's something animal about it. The other player may be thinking his own thoughts but he won't be able to help casting him a wary sideways glance—I've seen it again and again—and he'll be thinking, 'Oh, my God! This is Nadal, who fights for every point as if it were his last. Today I'm going to have to be at the very top of my game, I'm going to have to have the day of my life. And not to win, just to have a chance.'"

The performance is all the more dramatic in Roig's eyes for the chasm that separates Nadal the competitor "with that extra something real champions have" from Nadal the private man. "You know that a part of him is wracked by nerves, you know that in everyday life he is an ordinary guy—an unfailingly decent and nice guy— who can be unsure of himself and full of anxieties, but you see him there in the locker room and suddenly he is transforming himself before your very eyes into a conqueror."

But the Rafael his family saw emerge from the locker room onto the Centre Court was neither a conqueror nor an axe-wielding gladiator, nor a fighting bull. They were terrified for him. They knew he was brilliant and they knew he was brave and, while they would never let on, they were a little in awe of him, but what they were seeing now, as the contest was about to begin, was something altogether more humanly fragile.

Rafael Maymó is Nadal's shadow, his most intimate companion on the grindingly long global tennis circuit. Trim, neat, towered over by his six-foot-one friend and employer, the thirty-three-year-old Maymó is a discreet, shrewd, serene Mallorcan from Nadal's hometown of Manacor. Since he started working as Nadal's physical therapist in September 2006, the two have developed a relationship that is practically telepathic. They barely need to talk to understand each other, but Maymó—or Titín, as Nadal affectionately calls him, though the nickname has no meaning— has learned to tell when the mood is ripe for him to speak up, when to lend an ear. His role is not unlike that of a groom with a purebred racehorse. He rubs Nadal's muscles, tapes his joints, soothes his electric temperament. Maymó is Nadal's horse whisperer.

Maymó attends to Nadal's needs of the moment, psychological as well as physical, but he knows his limitations: he sees that these end where the family begins, for they are the pillar that sustains Nadal, as a person and as an athlete. "You cannot stress too much the significance of the family on his life," Maymó says. "Or how united he and they are. Each of Rafa's triumphs is indivisibly a triumph of the whole family. The parents, the sister, the uncles, the aunt, the grandparents: they act on the principle of one for all and all for one. They savor his victories and suffer his defeats. They are like a part of his body, as if they were an extension of Rafa's arm."

So many of them show up so often at Nadal's matches, Maymó says, because they understand he is not 100 percent fully functional without them. "It's not a duty. They need to be there. They see no choice in the matter. But they also feel that his chances of success will increase if, when he looks up at the crowds before a match begins, he sees them there. That is why when he wins a big victory, his instinct is to jump up into the stands to embrace them; or if any are back home watching on TV, the first thing he does back in the locker room is phone them."

His father, Sebastián Nadal, endured the most nerve-shredding experience of his life at the Centre Court on the day of the 2008 Wimbledon final. An image of what happened after the 2007 final, also against Federer, gnawed at Sebastián, as it did at the rest of the Nadal family. They all knew how Rafael had reacted after that five-set loss. Sebastián had described to them the scene in the Wimbledon locker room: Rafael sitting on the floor of the shower for half an hour, a picture of despair, the water that pounded his head blending with the tears that rolled down his cheeks.

"I was so afraid of another defeat—not for me, but for Rafael," said Sebastián, a big man who in his working life is a steady, calm entrepreneur. "I had that picture of him destroyed, utterly sunk, after the 2007 final, nailed inside my head and I did not want to have to see it again. And I thought, if he loses, what can I do—what can I possibly do—to make it less traumatic for him? That was the game of Rafael's life; that was the biggest day. I had a terrible time. I've never suffered so much."

All those closest to Nadal shared Sebastián's suffering that day; all saw the soft, vulnerable core hidden beneath the hard warrior shell.

Nadal's sister, Maribel, a lanky and good-humored college student, five years younger than he, is amused by the gap between the perception the public has of her brother and her own knowledge of him. An unusually overprotective big brother, who calls her or texts ten times a day, wherever in the world he might be, he gets into a terrible flap, she says, at the slightest suggestion that she might be falling ill. "One time when he was way in Australia my doctor ordered me to have some tests done—nothing too serious—but in all the messages I exchanged with Rafael that was the one thing I didn't mention. It would freak him out; it would risk throwing him completely off his game," says Maribel, whose pride in her brother's achievements does not blind her to "the truth," expressed with teasing affection, that he is "a bit of a scaredy cat."

Nadal's mother, Ana María Parera, does not disagree. "He's on top in the tennis world but, deep down, he is a super-sensitive human being full of fears and insecurities that people who don't know him would scarcely imagine," she says. "He doesn't like the dark, for example, and he prefers to sleep with the light, or the TV, on. He is not comfortable with thunder and lightning either. When he was a child he'd hide under a cushion when that happened and, even now, when there's a storm and you need to go outside to fetch something, he won't let you. And then there are his eating habits, his loathing of cheese and tomato, and of ham, the national dish of Spain. I'm not as mad about ham myself as most people seem to be, but cheese? It is a bit peculiar."

A fussy eater, he is also fussy behind the wheel of a car. Nadal enjoys driving, but maybe more in the make-believe world of his PlayStation, a constant companion when he is on tour, than in a real car. "He's a prudent driver," his mother says. "He accelerates, brakes, accelerates, brakes, and he is awfully careful about overtaking, however powerful his car might be."

Maribel, his sister, is more blunt than his mother. She describes Rafael as "a terrible driver." And she finds it funny too that, while loving the sea, he is also afraid of it. "He's always talking about buying himself a boat. He loves fishing and Jet Skiing, but he won't Jet Ski, nor will he swim, unless he can see the sand at the bottom. Nor will he ever dive off a high rock into the sea, as his friends do all the time."

But all these foibles are nothing compared to his most persistent anxiety: that something bad may happen to his family. Not only does he panic at the merest suggestion of ill health in the family, he is forever fretting that an accident may befall them. "I like to light up the fireplace almost every night," says his mother, at whose large, modern seafront home he still lives, in a wing of the house with its own bedroom, sitting room, and bathroom. "If he goes out, he'll remind me before leaving to put out the fire before I go to sleep. And then he'll phone three times from whatever restaurant or bar he is in to make sure I've done so. If I take the car to drive to Palma, only an hour away, he'll beg me, always, to drive slowly and carefully."

Ana María, a wise and strong Mediterranean matriarch, never ceases to be amazed by the incoherence between how brave he is on the tennis court and how fear-ridden off it. "He is a straightforward kind of person, at first sight," she says, "and also a very good person, but he is also full of ambiguities. If you know what he is like deep down, there are things about him that don't quite square."

That is why he has to arm himself with courage in the buildup to a big game, why he does what he does inside the locker room, willing himself into a personality change, bottling up his inherent fears and the nerves of the moment before releasing the gladiator within.

To the anonymous multitudes the man who emerged from the locker room onto the Centre Court for the start of the Wimbledon 2008 final was Superman; to his intimates, he was also Clark Kent. One was quite as real as the other; it might even be that one depended on the other. Benito Pérez Barbadillo, his press chief since December 2006, is as convinced that Nadal's insecurities are the fuel of his competitive fire as he is that his family offers him the core of affection and support necessary to keep them in check. Pérez worked in the tennis world for ten years, as an official at the Association of Tennis Professionals before becoming Nadal's press chief, and has known, in some cases very well, most of the top players of this period. Nadal, he believes, is different from the rest, as a player and as a man. "That unique mental strength and self-confidence and warrior spirit is the reverse side of the insecurity that drives him," he says. All his fears—be they of the dark, of thunderstorms, of the sea, or of the disastrous disruption of his family life—obey a compelling need. "He is a person who needs to be in control of everything," Pérez says, "but since this is impossible, he invests all he has in controlling the one part of his life over which he has most command, Rafa the tennis player."

CHAPTER 2

THE DYNAMIC DUO

T HE FIRST POINT is always important, more so in a Wimbledon final. I'd felt good, I'd had those good sensations all morning; now I had to prove it to myself on court. Federer got in a good first serve wide to my backhand. I clawed the return back, better than he expected, deeper. He was preparing himself to move in behind that serve, using the forward momentum of the body to add power to his shot; but my return wrong-footed him, obliged him to shuffle back a couple of steps and hit the ball uncomfortably high on his forehand, on the back foot, limiting him to the power of his arm alone. It was a better return than I might have reasonably expected to a deep and difficult serve, one that immediately got him thinking, adjusting.

Break that easy rhythm of his, push him to the edge—that's what I have to do against Federer, always. That's what Toni said right back the very first time I played him, in Miami, five years earlier: "You're not going to beat him on talent, on the brilliance of your shot-making. He'll always be more able to make a winner out of nothing than you. So you have to press him all the time, force him to play at the very limit of his abilities." Even though I won that first match of ours in Miami 6–3, 6–3, Toni was right. His serve is better than mine, his volley too; his forehand is probably more decisive than mine, his sliced backhand definitely is, and his positioning on the court is better too. There was a reason why he had been world number one for the previous five years and I had been number two for the previous four. Besides, Federer had won Wimbledon the last five years in a row. He practically owned the place. I knew I had to beat him mentally if I was to win. The strategy with Federer is never to let up, to try and wear him down from the first point to the last.

Federer struck that awkward first return of mine well to my backhand, and I tried to hit the ball back to his—applying the game plan right from the beginning—but he played around it, took it on the forehand. But now I had the initiative, I was in the center of the court, he'd had to push out wider. Then his forehand to my backhand, but he did not hit it too deep, allowing me to steer the ball straight and deep down the line, with no chance this time for him to play around the backhand. Federer angled the ball diagonally across to my forehand and I saw my chance to go for the winner. With him expecting to receive again on his backhand, I whipped the ball toward his forehand corner. The ball dropped just inside the baseline and spun, high and wide, beyond his reach.

A first point like that gives you confidence. You're feeling in tune with the surface, you feel you're controlling the ball and not that it is controlling you. On that point I had control of the ball in every one of the seven shots I hit. That gives you peace of mind. The nerves are working for you, not against you. It's what you need at the start of a Wimbledon final.

A funny thing about Wimbledon: despite the grandeur of the place and the weight of expectations it generates, of all tournaments it is the one where I am able to recreate the calmest sense of home. Instead of staying in some vast hotel suite—some of the places where they put me up make me laugh, they can be so needlessly extravagant—I live in a rented house across the road from the All England Club. A normal house, nothing fancy, but big enough— three floors—for my family, my team, and friends to stay or come round for dinner. It gives this tournament a whole different feel from all the others. Instead of each of us being isolated in our hotel rooms we have a space we can all share; instead of having to drive through traffic to the courts in an official car, a two-minute walk and you're there. Being in a house also means we have to do our own food shopping. When I can, I go to the local supermarket to buy a few of the things that I eat far too much of, like Nutella chocolate, or potato chips, or olives. I am not a model of healthy eating, not for a professional athlete anyway. I eat as normal people do. If I feel like something, I'll have it. I'm especially mad about olives. In and of themselves they're OK, not like chocolate or chips. But my problem is the quantities I eat. My mother often reminds me of the time when, as a small child, I hid inside a cupboard and devoured a huge jar of olives, so many I vomited and was sick for days. The experience might have changed my attitude to olives, but it didn't and never has. I crave olives and I'm not happy when I find myself somewhere where they are hard to find.

I found them in Wimbledon but I had to be careful over the timing of my trips to buy them. If I went when the supermarket was crowded I ran the risk of being mobbed for autographs. This is an occupational hazard that I accept and I try to take it with good grace. I can't say "no" to people who ask me for my signature, even to the rude ones who just stick a piece of paper in front of me and don't even say "please." I'll sign for them too, but what they won't get from me is a smile. So going to the supermarket in Wimbledon, while an enjoyable distraction from the tension of competition, does have its pressures. The only place where I can go shopping in peace—where I can do anything like a normal person—is my home town of Manacor.

The one soothing similarity between Wimbledon and Manacor is that house we all stay in and the pleasure of that short stroll to the courts, which reminds me of when I started playing tennis, at the age of four. We lived in an apartment opposite the town's tennis club, and I'd cross the road and train with my uncle Toni, the resident coach.

The clubhouse is what you'd expect in a town of barely forty thousand people. Medium-sized, dominated by a large restaurant with a terrace overhanging the courts, all clay. One day I joined in with a group of half a dozen children Toni was teaching. I liked it right from the start. I was already crazy about football, playing on the streets with my friends every spare moment my parents let me, and anything that involved a ball was going to be fun. I liked football best. I liked being part of a team. Toni says that at first I found tennis boring. But being in a group helped, and it's what made possible everything that followed. If it had just been me and my uncle it would have been too suffocating. It wasn't till I was thirteen, when I knew my future was in tennis, that he began training me on my own.

Toni was tough on me right from the start, tougher than on the other children. He demanded a lot of me, pressured me hard. He'd use rough language, he'd shout a lot, he'd frighten me—especially when the other boys didn't turn up and it was just the two of us. If I saw I'd be alone with him when I arrived for training, I'd get a sinking feeling in my stomach. Miguel Ángel Munar, still today one of my best friends, would come there two or three times a week; me, four or five times. We'd play between one fifteen and two thirty, during our lunch break from school. And sometimes after school too, when I didn't have football practice. Miguel Ángel reminds me sometimes how Toni , if he saw my head was wandering, would belt the ball hard at me, not to hit me, but to scare me, to startle me to attention. At that age, as Miguel Ángel says, all our heads wandered, but mine was the one that was allowed to wander least. It was always me too that he got to pick up the balls, or more balls than the others, at the end of the training session; and it was me who had to sweep the courts when we were done for the day. Anyone who might have expected any favoritism on his part was mistaken. Quite the opposite. Miguel Ángel says he bluntly discriminated against me, knowing he could not have gotten away with it with him and the other boys but with me he could, because I was his nephew.

On the other hand, he always encouraged me to think for myself on the tennis court. I've seen reports in the news media saying that Toni forced me to play left-handed, and that he did this because it would make me harder to play against. Well, it's not true. It's a story the newspapers have made up. The truth is that I began playing when I was very small, and because I wasn't strong enough to hit the ball over the net, I'd hold the racket with both hands, on the forehand as well as the backhand. Then one day my uncle said, "There are no professional players who play with two hands and we're not going to be the first ones, so you've got to change." So I did, and what came naturally to me was to play left-handed. Why, I can't tell. Because I write with my right hand, and when I play basketball or golf—or darts—I play right-handed too. But in football I play with my left; my left foot is much stronger than my right. People say this gives me an advantage on the double-handed backhand, and that may be right. Having more feeling, more control on both hands than the majority of players, has to work in my favor, especially on cross-court shots, where a little extra strength helps. But this was definitely not something that Toni, in a moment of genius, thought up. It's dumb to imagine that he might have been able to force me to play in a way that did not come naturally to me.

But, yes, Toni was hard on me. My mother remembers that as a small child sometimes I'd come home from training crying. She'd try to get me to tell her what the matter was, but I preferred to keep quiet. Once I confessed to her that Toni had a habit of calling me a "mummy's boy," which pained her, but I begged her not to say anything to Toni, because that would only have made matters worse.

Toni never let up. Once I started playing competitive games, when I was seven, it got tougher. One very hot day I went to a match without my bottle of water. I'd forgotten it back home. He could have gone and bought me one, but he didn't. So that I'd learn to take responsibility, he said. Why didn't I rebel? Because I enjoyed tennis, and enjoyed it all the more once I started winning, and because I was an obedient and docile child. My mother says I was too easy to manipulate. Maybe, but if I hadn't loved playing the game, I wouldn't have put up with my uncle. And I loved him too, as I still do and always will. I trusted him, and so I knew deep down that he was doing what he thought was best for me.

I trusted him to the point that, for several years, I believed the tall stories he would tell me about his sporting prowess, winning the Tour de France, for instance, or starring as a football player in Italy. I trusted him so implicitly when I was little that I even came to believe he had supernatural powers. It wasn't till I was nine years old that I stopped thinking he was a magician capable, among other things, of making himself invisible. During family get-togethers my father and grandfather would play along with him on this, pretend to me that they couldn't see him. So I came to believe that I could see him but other people couldn't. Toni even convinced me he had the power to make rain.

One day when I was seven, I was playing in a match against a boy of twelve. We didn't rate our chances very highly, so Toni told me before the game that if I went down 0–5, he'd bring on the rain so the game would have to be called off. Well, as I saw it at the time, he lost faith too soon. Because the rain started falling when I was down 0–3. Then I won the next two games and suddenly I felt confident about my chances. So I went up to my uncle during the changeover at 2–3 and I said, "I think you can stop the rain now. I reckon I can beat this guy." A couple of games later the rain stopped, and in the end I lost 7–5. But two more years had to pass before I stopped believing my uncle was a rainmaker.

So there was fun and magic in my relationship with Toni, even if the prevailing mood when we trained was stony and severe. And we had plenty of success. If he hadn't made me play without water that day, if he hadn't singled me out for especially harsh treatment when I was in that group of little kids learning the game, if I hadn't cried as I did at the injustice and abuse he heaped on me, maybe I would not be the player I am today. He always stressed the importance of endurance. "Endure, put up with whatever comes your way, learn to overcome weakness and pain, push yourself to breaking point but never cave in. If you don't learn that lesson, you'll never succeed as an elite athlete": that was what he taught me.

Often I'd struggle to contain my rage. "Why is it me and not the other boys who have to sweep the court after training?" I'd ask myself. "Why do I have to pick up more balls than the other? Why does he scream at me that way when I hit the ball out?" But I learned to internalize that anger too, not to fret at the injustice, to accept it and get on with it. Yes, he might have gone too far, but it's worked very well for me. All that tension in every single coaching session, right from the very start, has allowed me today to face up to the difficult moments in a match with more self-control than might otherwise have been the case. Toni did a lot to build that fighting character people say they see in me on court.

But my values as a person and my way of being, which ultimately is what underlines my game, come from my father and mother. It's true that Toni has insisted I have to behave well on court, set an example, never throw a racket to the floor in anger, something I have never, ever done. But—and this is the point—if I had been brought up differently at home, I might not have paid him any attention. My parents always imposed a lot of discipline on me. They were very proper about things like table manners—"Don't talk with your mouth full!" "Sit up straight!"—about the need to be courteous and polite to everybody—say "good morning" and "good afternoon" to people we meet, shake hands with everybody. Both my parents and, for that matter, my uncle Toni have always said that, never mind the tennis, their biggest desire was that I should grow up to be "good people." My mother says that if I were not, if I behaved like a spoiled brat, she would still love me, but she'd be too embarrassed to travel halfway around the world to watch me play. They drummed into me the importance of treating everybody with respect from an early age. Whenever our team lost a football match, my father insisted that I had to go up to the players of the rival team afterward and congratulate them. I had to say to each one of them something like "Well done, champ. Very well played." I didn't like it. I felt miserable when we lost, and my face must have showed that my heart wasn't in the words I was saying. But I knew I'd get into trouble if I didn't do as my father said, so I did it. And the habit stayed with me. It comes naturally to me to praise an opponent after he's beaten me, or even if I've won, if he deserves it.

For all the discipline, I had an amazingly happy and warm family life as a child, and maybe that is why I was able to put up with the harsh treatment I received from Toni. One balanced the other out, because above all what my parents gave me was an incredible feeling of security. My father, Sebastián, is the oldest of my grandparents' five children and I was the first grandchild. This meant that I was fussed over by my three uncles and my aunt, who had no children of their own then, as well as by my grandparents, right from my very first days. They tell me that I was the family mascot, their "favorite toy." My father says that when I was only fifteen days old, he and my mother would leave me to stay overnight at my grandparents', where my uncles and my aunt still lived. When I was a baby and then later when I was a child of two and three, they'd take me with them to the bar where they met their friends, chatted, and played cards or billiards or Ping Pong. Mixing in adult company became the most natural thing in the world for me. I have unforgettably warm memories of those times. My aunt Marilén, who is also my godmother, would take me to the beach in Porto Cristo, just ten minutes away from Manacor, which is inland, and I'd lie on her tummy, dozing in the sun. With my uncles I'd play football in the corridor of the apartment, or down in the garage. One of my uncles, Miguel Ángel, was a professional footballer. He played for Mallorca, and later for Barcelona and for Spain. When I was very small, they'd take me along to the stadium to watch him play. For all the haranguing I got from Toni, I am not one of those athletes whose life stories are all about overcoming dark beginnings in their rise to the top. I had a fairy tale childhood.

One thing I do seem to have in common with everyone I've ever heard about who has succeeded in sports is a fanatical competitive edge. As a little boy I'd hate losing at anything. Cards, a little football game in the garage, whatever. I'd throw fits of rage if I lost; I still do. Just a couple of years ago I lost at cards with my family and I went so far as to accuse the others of cheating, which I now see was going a little too far. I don't know where all that comes from. Maybe from watching my uncles compete in the bar at billiards with their friends. Yet it used to amaze even them that, sweet as I supposedly was, I became transformed into a little demon whenever there was a game on.

On the other hand, the desire to succeed—linked to the knowledge that you have to work hard to fulfill your ambitions—definitely can be traced to my family. On my mother's side, they own a furniture business in Manacor, the furniture industry having long been the heart of the town's economy. My grandfather's father died when he was ten, and from an early age he learned the family craft. He became a master furniture maker. In my mother's house, where I live, we still have an incredibly fine chest of drawers that he made with his own hands. My grandfather tells me that in the year 1970, two thousand beds were made in Mallorca and the neighboring Balearic Islands of Ibiza and Menorca. Half of them were made in his workshops. One of my uncles, my godfather, runs the business now.

The genetic influence on me is even more clear on my father's side of the family. Not that a passion for sports has always been what defines them. My grandfather, also called Rafael, is a musician. A story he has told us many times reveals what an incredibly single-minded and driven person he was when he was still young. When he was sixteen—he is in his eighties now and going very strong, still working in music, doing opera with children—he set up and directed a choir in town. A serious choir, so serious that when he was nineteen, the head of what was then the newly formed symphonic orchestra of Mallorca—we're talking the late 1940s now— came to him and asked him if he could prepare his choir for a performance of Beethoven's Ninth Symphony in Palma, the island's capital. This was not long after the Spanish Civil War and the country was very poor. It was an amazingly ambitious enterprise. All the more so because, of the eighty-four members of the choir, only half a dozen knew how to read music. The rest were amateurs. But my grandfather did not let this deter him. They rehearsed every single day for six and a half months, and, as he says, "the day came when a Mallorcan heard Beethoven's Ninth for the first time, live, inside a theater." It was, as he tells it, a famous day in the island's history. It would not have happened without him. And he was only nineteen.

I think it might have been a little disappointing for him that none of his five children showed any aptitude for music, and surprising that three of them should have turned out to be gifted at sports. Not my father, though. He's a businessman, heart and soul; one of those who doesn't just do it for the money, but for the thrill of it too. He loves making deals, setting up companies, creating jobs. He's always been this way.

One summer when he was sixteen he set up a bar in Porto Cristo, the beach resort nearest to Manacor, where he organized musical events. From the proceeds he bought himself his first motorbike.

When he was nineteen, he saw an opportunity in the used cars business. He found that agents were charging a lot of money for the paperwork needed to change the ownership of vehicles, so he figured out how to offer the service at a better price. He worked as a bank employee for a short while, got bored, and then, through a friend of his father—who aside from his music had a sideline in real estate—he got involved in a glass-making business in Manacor. They cut the glass for windows, tables, and doors. The business went well because of a tourism boom in Mallorca, and in two years my father raised a loan, with my uncle Toni as his partner, and bought out the company. Toni had no talent for, or interest in, business, so my father did all the work, allowing Toni to dedicate himself full-time to his tennis coaching, and to me. Today my father is as busy as he ever has been. He's still involved in the glass business; he has interests in real estate and he helps explore potentially lucrative investments on my behalf. Thanks to the good luck I've had and the contacts I've made, he is operating at a higher level of business, internationally, than ever before. He doesn't need to do this for himself, but he does it for me, and also because he enjoys it. He doesn't stop; he can never have enough new challenges, which is maybe one reason why in the family they all say I take after my father.

The sporty uncles were Toni, who played professional tennis before becoming a coach; Rafael, who played football in a Mallorcan league for several years; and Miguel Ángel, who made it to the very top in football. His big break came when he signed, aged nineteen, for Mallorca, a club that played in the Spanish first division. The actual day when he signed the contract (with my father acting as his agent) was the day I was born, June 3, 1986. Miguel Ángel was a tall, strong, intelligent, all-terrain player, as capable of playing in defense as in midfield. And he scored a fair number of goals too. Anyone who is impressed by my physical condition or my hard work and perseverance should look at him: he carried on playing professional football at the highest level to the age of thirty-eight. He played sixty-two times for the Spanish national team and more than three hundred times in eight seasons for Barcelona, during which time he won five national league championships and the biggest trophy in club football, the European Cup. I went to watch him play often, but I especially remember him taking me to Barcelona's Camp Nou stadium, the largest in Europe, when I was ten, to play with half a dozen members of the first team after their official training session had ended. I wore a Barcelona shirt that day. A long time would pass before my family stopped teasing me about that because, despite adoring my uncle Miguel Ángel, I have always been and always will be a Real Madrid fan. As everybody knows, Real and Barça are the two most bitter rivals in world football. Why am I a Real fan? Simple. Because my father is, which gives you the measure of how great his influence has been on me as a person.

Every member of my family has contributed to who I am now. In the case of my uncle Miguel Ángel, I was lucky to get a taste of the kind of life that would await me after I made the grade as a tennis player. He was a big star, especially in Mallorca. In sports, along with the tennis player Carlos Moyá, who was once ranked number one in the world, he was the island's pride. My uncle was a great example to me. He gave me a glimpse of the life I was to live: he made money and he became famous; he appeared in the media, and he was mobbed and cheered wherever he went. But he never took himself too seriously; he never *believed* it—he never felt he truly deserved all the adulation he received—and he always remained a modest and straightforward person. That for me he always remained just my uncle meant that I also learned from a young age to put all that celebrity stuff in perspective and, when the time came, to keep my feet on the ground. Miguel Ángel gave practical, flesh-and-blood solidity to the lessons in humility my uncle Toni and my parents taught me early on in my life. I'm very much aware now that everything that's happened to me is not because of *who* I am, but because of *what* I do. There is a difference. There's Rafa Nadal the tennis player who people see triumphing, and there's me, Rafael, the person, the same as I always was and the same as I would have been whatever I'd done with my life, whether I'd become well known or not. Miguel Ángel's also been important for my family: the experience with him prepared them for the experience with me. They were able to cope with my fame more easily and naturally than they might have otherwise.

Miguel Ángel, now assistant coach at Mallorca Football Club, in the Spanish first division, points out to me these days that other people whose family members have been famous let things go to their heads when they themselves become well known. He says that, quite apart from anything he might have done, my parents and Toni are the ones who prepared me to deal with all the trappings of celebrity, and he praises me for having shown the intelligence to learn those lessons well. Miguel Ángel also believes that I am not fully conscious of the magnitude of what I have achieved. He may be right and, if so, it is probably just as well.

Things might have turned out very differently for me if I'd opted to play football for a living instead of tennis. Football was the game all kids played in Mallorca, whether they had a family connection with the sport or not. I took the game deadly seriously. Miguel Ángel lived at home with my grandparents in the early years of his professional career. When he had a game the next day, I'd say to him the night before, "Come on! We've got to train! We have to win tomorrow!" And with great solemnity, at ten at night, me just four years old, I'd lead him and my uncle Rafael down to the garage for a session of hard running, with and without the ball. It's comical thinking about it now, but I think that awareness of the importance of preparing hard for success in sport reinforced in me the idea I've always had that you get as much out of your game as you put into it.

Football was my passion as a child, and remains so today. I can be at a tournament in Australia or Bangkok, and if there is a big Real Madrid game on TV at five in the morning, I'll wake up to watch it—even, sometimes, if I have a match on later that day. And I'll build my day's training program, if need be, around the timing of the games. I'm a fanatic. My godfather remembers when I was four years old, how he would show me pictures of the shields of all the teams in the Spanish first division, and—to his amazement—I'd be able to put a name correctly to all of them. Playing at any level, even if it was just a little game in the garage with one of my uncles, I'd get terribly angry if I lost. And I never wanted to stop. My uncle Rafael still recalls, with some pain, the times when I'd stay at his home on Friday night and then wake him up at nine thirty, when he'd gone to bed the night before at five, to get him to come out and play with me. I always managed to convince him. A part of him hated me at the time, but he tells me he found it impossible to resist my enthusiasm. These days I'm on the receiving end. I am the oldest of thirteen cousins, and it is they now who wake me up to play after a long night out. But I'm always up for it. Because I just enjoy it so much and because I never forget how seriously I took the game as a child, especially after I started playing for the local Manacor team competitively in a kids' league at the age of seven.

My dad and Miguel Ángel enjoy reminding me how after each

of my matches I'd analyze the plays as studiously as we did my
uncle's first division games. I'd discuss my failings as well as my
goals, which I scored a lot of from my position on the left wing of
the attack (about fifty a season), despite being the youngest member
of the team by a year. We trained all week, and on the night before a
match I'd be a bag of nerves. I'd wake up at six in the morning to
think through the game and prepare myself mentally for it. Partly
to calm my nerves, I'd always clean and polish my boots before a
match. My mother and sister chuckle when they remember this, because they say that when it comes to sports I am a disciplined and
orderly person, but in everything else I am distracted and chaotic.
They are right. My room at home is always a mess—my hotel room
when I am traveling too—and I often forget things. All my focus is
on the game I am playing, as it was back then before a big match. I'd
visualize the game ahead, imagine goals I might score and passes I
might make. I'd limber up in my room. I'd prepare almost as intensely as I do before a big tennis match now, and with as much tension. Looking back on it now, it's funny, but then it was the world to
me. More important than tennis, at first, for all the intensity of my
sessions with Toni and the belief he transmitted to me that I'd play
for a living one day. My dream then, like so many boys my age in
Spain, was to be a professional footballer. Even though I was playing
competitive tennis too, from the age of seven, and doing well, I always got more nervous before a football match. I guess it was because I wasn't playing for myself alone; I felt a sense of responsibility
toward my teammates.

I also had a blind faith in our capacity to win games, even when
all seemed lost. My uncles remind me how I was always so much
more convinced of our chances than the rest of the boys on our team,
how there were games when we were losing 5–0 and I'd be there in

the locker room yelling, "Let's not give up! We can still win this!" Or the time when we lost 6–0 away in Palma, and on the way back I said, "It doesn't matter. When we play them at home, we'll win."

But there were more victories than defeats. I remember lots of games vividly. I remember, in particular, the season we won the Balearic Islands championship, when I was eleven years old. The decisive game was against Mallorca, the big team from the capital of the island. We were losing 1–0 at halftime but came back to win 2–1. A penalty decided the game for us. It was a run I made into the penalty area that provoked a player on the other team into handling the ball right on the goal line. The normal thing would have been for me to take the penalty, as I was the team's top goal scorer, but I didn't dare. You look at me now playing a Wimbledon final and you maybe wonder why not. Well, strength of character is something I've had to work on. Taking on that responsibility was too much for me at that moment. Luckily, my teammate scored. The joy of winning that championship was as great as the joy of winning a Grand Slam tennis tournament. It may sound strange, but the two are comparable. At that moment it was the greatest thing to which I could aspire. It was the same excitement and sense of triumph, only on a smaller stage.

I don't think there is anything in any area of life that gives you the same rush as winning in sport, whatever the sport and at whatever the level. There is no feeling as intense or as joyous. And the more you crave winning, the greater the rush when you succeed.

My first taste of that in tennis came when I was eight and won the championship of the Balearic Islands in the under-12s category. That ranks for me, still today, as one of the greatest victories of my career. A difference of four years at that age feels like an eternity; the older children in my category seemed like distant, higher beings. That was why I entered the tournament with no notion at all that I might win. I'd only won one tournament up until then, and it was against children my own age. But by now, and for over a year, I'd been training with Toni practically an hour and a half a day, five days a week, every week. I don't imagine any other boy competing in that tournament trained as much as I did, or with as hard a coach. I also think that, with Toni's help, I had a better understanding of the game than other kids. That's what gave me the edge, and maybe still does.

If you watch the number ten player in the world and the number five hundred in training, you won't necessarily be able to tell who is higher up in the rankings. Without the pressure of competition, they'll move and hit the ball much the same way. But really knowing how to play is not only about striking the ball well, it's about making the right choices, about knowing when you should go for a drop shot or hit the ball hard, or high, or deep, when you play with backspin or topspin or flat, and where in the court you should aim to hit it. Toni made me think a lot about the basic tactics of tennis from an early age. If I messed up, Toni would ask, "Where did you go wrong?" And we'd talk about it, analyze my mistakes at length. Far from seeking to make me his puppet, he strove to make me think for myself. Toni said tennis was a game in which you had to process a lot of information very fast; you had to think better than your rival to succeed. And to think straight, you had to keep your cool.

By pushing me always to the edge, he built up my mental strength, an effort that paid dividends in the quarter finals of that first under-12s championship I played, in a match where my rival was the favorite, a boy three years older than me. I lost the first three games without winning a point but ended up winning in straight sets. I won the final in two sets too. I've still got the cup at home, on display alongside the trophies I've won as a professional.

It was a very important victory, for it provided me with the impetus for everything that followed. But the setting was far from grand. For the final, in the neighboring island of Ibiza, about fifty people turned up—most of them my family members. They were happy when I won, I remember, but nothing over the top. No wild celebrations afterward: that is not our style. Some kids, in tennis as in other sports, are driven by the ambition of their parents, usually their fathers. I had Toni. But the intensity of his desire for me to triumph was complemented in a healthy way by my father's relaxed attitude to the whole thing. He was far, far removed from those parents who aspire to achieve their lives' frustrated dreams through the success of their children. He drove me to games up and down and across Mallorca every weekend—for which I can never thank him enough—and he stayed to watch me play, not because he wanted me to be a star but because he wanted me to be happy. It never crossed his mind in those days that I'd end up being a professional tennis player, never mind that I'd win what I've won.

There's an anecdote from my childhood my father and I both remember well that reveals his attitude toward me and my attitude toward tennis, and how different each was. It was two years after I'd won the Balearic Islands championship, just after the summer vacation, in September. I'd had a really fun August with my friends, fishing, swimming in the sea, playing football on the beach. But I hadn't trained much, and then, suddenly, I was playing in a tournament in Palma. My father drove me there, as usual, and I lost. I still remember the score: 6–3, 6–3, against a guy I should have beaten. On the way back home in the car I was deathly silent. My father, who'd never seen me so gloomy, tried to cheer me up. He said, "Come on. It's not such a big deal. Don't feel bad. You can't always win." I said nothing. He couldn't shake me out of my dark mood. So he went on. "Look. You've had a fantastic summer with your friends. Be happy with that. You can't have everything. You can't be a slave to tennis." He thought he was presenting me with a convincing argument, but I burst out crying, which shocked him still more because I never cried. Not then. He insisted. "Come on, you've had a terrific summer. Why's that not enough?" "Yes, Dad," I replied, "but all the fun I had then can't make up for the pain I'm feeling right now. I never want to feel this way again."

My father repeats those words to this day, and he is still stunned that I should have said something so perceptive, and so prescient, at such a young age. He sees that exchange we had in the car as a defining moment, as a day in which his understanding of his son changed, and my understanding of my ambitions in life changed too. I grasped that the one thing that upset me above all other things was the feeling that I had let myself down, that I had lost without giving my best. Instead of driving back home, he took me to a restaurant by the sea to eat what was then my favorite food, fried shrimp. We didn't talk much as we ate, but we both knew a bridge had been crossed. Something had been said that would define and shape me for a long time to come.

Eleven years later, in 2007, I relived that same sense of despair after losing the Wimbledon final to Roger Federer. As the tears fell, I thought, "I never want to feel this way again." And I thought that again, but in a much more collected and constructive frame of mind, at the start of the rematch in 2008.

Winning that first point on Federer's serve, and winning it well, was the first step in curing a hurt I'd been carrying for twelve months. But then, on the second point, after a decent rally ended with me going for the winner too soon and hitting a rather wild forehand out, it was back to the beginning. That's tennis. You play a great point, you win with a fine shot at the end of a long and tense rally, but that has no more value in the final score than the gift of a point I gave him here. That's where the mental strength comes in, what separates champions from near champions. You put that failure immediately behind you, clean out of your mind. You do not allow your mind to dwell on it. You draw, instead, on the strength of having won the first point and build on that, thinking only of what comes next.

The problem was that all too quickly he began to show why he was the best in the world. He won the game with a bullet of a diagonally angled backhand, with a forehand drive down the line and with an ace. I went back to my chair the wiser and, in the long run, the stronger for having received an instant reminder that this was not going to be a repeat of the easy win I'd had over him in the French Open only twenty-eight days earlier; and a reminder too that Federer's serve, on a grass surface that benefits the big servers, was much better than mine.

He won that first game at 15, but there was some consolation, and much to sustain my belief in victory. Though I'd lost four of the five points, we'd had long rallies in each, in all of which I had been timing the ball well. He'd had to fight to win his serve. The disadvantage was that now I'd have to come from behind, possibly for the duration of the set, to remain on level terms.

Things went better than I had expected. The plan was to serve to his backhand corner, which I did on every point in the second game, and practically every service point throughout. The fourth point of that game encouraged me to continue in that vein. I served to his backhand; he hit a high, sliced return, which I hit deep to his backhand again; then the same again and again, hitting the ball with top spin high and deep to his backhand, pinning him back uncomfortably. Four balls, one after the other, on the same spot and high to his left. That gave him little option each time but to float a slice back to the center of the court, giving me time to get into position and place the ball exactly where I wanted it to go. If I had hit to his forehand, he would have risked a flatter, stronger return and I might have lost control of the point. That way, I did control the point, which ended with him losing his cool for a critical instant and going for a backhand drive that flew high and way off course. I wasn't going to win every point this way, but here was a clear signal that this was a plan I had to stick to.

And next game, the breakthrough. Federer had only lost two service games in six matches on his way to the final; this would be his third. I won one point with a shot deep to his forehand corner, but otherwise kept pinning him back on the backhand side. Three times there he fluffed his shots. I was 2–1 up, next up to serve, and, for now, winning the psychological battle, which usually translates into you playing better than your opponent, because you're thinking more clearly. I felt satisfied but not elated. There was a long road ahead, and any thought of victory, any hint now of a movie with a happy ending entering my head, would have been suicide. What I had to do was keep focused and transmit to him by my actions and my demeanor that I was not going to flag on any point. If he wanted to beat me, he'd have to play every single point well, very well; not only would he have to be at the top of his game, he'd have to be at the top of his game for a long time. My objective now was to convey to him that he was going to have to spend hours stretched to the limit.

He got the message. He did not let up again. But it was too late. We both played at our best to the very end of the first set, but I held all my service games and won it 6—4.

UNCLE TONI

ASK TONI NADAL what his last words were to his nephew before he left the Wimbledon locker room at the start of the 2008 final and he'll tell you: "I told him to battle to the end and endure." Ask him why Rafa has made it to the top of world tennis and he'll reply: "Because it's all in the head, in your attitude, in wanting more, in enduring more than your rival." Ask him what he says to Rafa on those days when the body rebels and the pain seems too great to compete on court, and his reply will be: "I say to him, 'Look, you've got two roads to choose from: tell yourself you've had enough and we leave, or be prepared to suffer and keep going. The choice is between enduring and giving up.'"

"Endurance" is a word Toni has been hammering into Nadal's skull from a very early age. It expresses a Spartan philosophy of life uncommon on an island, and in a country, where the pleasure principle reigns. Toni comes across as a Spaniard from an earlier age, as if he were descended from Hernán Cortés, the sixteenth-century conquistador who landed in Mexico with a force of barely a hundred men, burned his boats so no one would be tempted to flee for home, and, after overcoming appalling privations and outrageous odds, defeated the Aztec empire, claiming its treasure and vast lands for the Spanish crown.

Toni, chunkily built and swarthy, with thick, powerful legs, looks like good conquistador material. Cold-eyed and resolute, he is a straight-speaker who makes little visible effort to ingratiate himself with those around him. He is not unkind: in the eyes of his family, he is generous to a fault with strangers who ask him for tickets to matches or with journalists needing a quote. But toward those closest to him, while unbendingly loyal, he can be moody, gruff, and quarrelsome. He is not the black sheep of the family, because ostracism is not something the tight-knit Nadals do. As Carlos Costa, who knows the Nadal family well, says, "Toni is different." He is grumpier than his brothers, more contrary; he is a moralizer, stiffly opinionated, always up for an argument.

But he is not quite as tough, or as self-sufficient a conquistador, as appearances might suggest. There has been a tendency in some of the sports media to suggest that Rafa would be nothing without Toni. One could make the opposite case: that Toni would be nothing without Rafa. The truth, though, lies in the middle. Toni and Rafa are a mutually dependent duo whose strengths and weaknesses complement each other. They are more powerful together than each would be on his own.

Toni once dreamt he might become a tennis champion. He excelled at the game in his youth, establishing a name for himself as one of Mallorca's finest. He was also the island's best table tennis player for a while, as well as a chess player of local repute. He had the body and he had the brains, but when he became a tennis professional and left home to try to conquer the Spanish mainland, he discovered that, while a steady player, he lacked the killer punch, which was precisely the quality he strove hardest to imbue in his young charges when he took up coaching. Boys whom he taught alongside his nephew recall that whereas other coaches highlighted the need to control the ball, Toni's emphasis was always on the aggressive cultivation of winners. Toni himself cites the example of the golfer Jack Nicklaus saying once in a coaching video that his advice to young players was "First, hit the ball far; then we'll think about getting it in the hole." Toni took the lesson to heart. His advice to his nephew, right from the start, when he was four years old, was "First, hit the ball hard; then we'll see about keeping it in."

And then he set about the more challenging task of constructing a mentally armor-plated competitor. He began, as he meant to continue, by treating his nephew with undisguised injustice in the company of his peers, while requiring him never to complain. The boys Nadal trained with recall that when Toni bellowed an order to him, made him stay behind and pick up the balls, then sweep the courts after training, he would bow his head and do as he was told. When the two trained alone, and the sun shone glaringly on one half of the court, that was the half where Toni would tell Rafa to play. If at the start of a session they were playing with good, sound balls, Toni would unexpectedly produce a bad one, a bare one that bounced erratically, or a soggy, lifeless one that hardly bounced at all. If his nephew complained, Toni would say, "The balls might be third rate but you're fourth rate!"

Cruel to be kind, as Toni saw it, he would play games with Rafa in which the winner was the first to twenty points. He would allow the excited child to get to nineteen, and then he'd raise his game, beating him to the post, ruining his nephew's day just as he was beginning to savor the thrill of an unlikely little victory. The blows to morale and the relentlessly harsh discipline to which he submitted Rafa all had a grand strategic purpose: teaching him to endure.

Toni's own relationship with the principle of "endurance," on the other hand, has been contradictory. Toni and his brother Sebastián first had impressed upon them the virtues of endurance during their teens, when they were away at boarding school in Palma, an hour's drive from Manacor. The school principal would preach to the pupils at length on the benefits of accepting life's inevitable trials and disappointments with manly resilience. The most immediate trial the brothers had to submit to was the harsh fact of boarding school existence itself, away from their unusually close, unusually nurturing family. Sebastián lasted the course. He stayed on at the school until the end of his appointed time. Toni lasted a year, after which he begged his parents to be allowed to return back home, and they consented. Later he began studying law and history at university but dropped out before obtaining his degree. After giving up on his quest to become a successful professional tennis player, he returned home to Manacor to coach children at the town's club.

Here he settled, having at last found his calling and, by spectacular good fortune, a nephew who possessed a mettle and a God-given ability he had not discovered in any other child before, or ever would again. From the way Rafa struck the ball, from his natural sense of positioning and from his strength of will, Toni quickly formed the impression that he had on his hands a future champion of Spain. Fate had arrived at the family doorstep, and he would make the most of it, drawing on the lessons he had learned from his own mistakes to instill in his nephew the habits of a winner, helping him forge a future in whose glories he would be able legitimately to share.

Rafa's success has given Toni a strong sense of vindication, encouraging him to become immensely forthright in his views, as severe in his certitudes as a black-clad Catholic in the Spanish court during the age of Cortés. But he seeks no comfort in the afterlife or in a benevolent divinity. No Catholic himself, he is as adamant as he is on all matters that religion is weakness and tomfoolery. He dismisses faith in God as a primitive magical belief as infantile as his nephew's former belief in his uncle's power to make rain.

Where Toni is unbendingly doctrinaire, however, is in his views regarding the way children should be brought up. "The problem nowadays," he says, "is that children have become too much the center of attention. Their parents, their families, everybody around them feels a need to put them on a pedestal. So much effort is invested in boosting their self-esteem that they are made to feel special in and of themselves, without having done anything. People get confused: they fail to grasp that you are not special because of who you are but because of what you do.

"I see it all the time, and then, if it turns out that they make money and acquire a little fame and everything is made easy for them and no one ever contradicts them, they are accommodated in every little detail of life, well . . . you end up with the most unbearable spoiled brats."

The phenomenon is so common in professional sports that the surprise comes, in Toni's view, when a brilliant young sportsman turns out to behave not like a brat but like an ordinary decent human being. Fawned upon, surrounded by grasping yes men, sports figures are told all the time they are gods, and they come to believe it. Rafa Nadal's feet-on-the-ground civility, such a departure from the expected norm, never ceases to be remarked upon, and Toni is proud of that.

Everything in the way Rafa Nadal was brought up prepared

him to behave in this way. Were he to end up a superstar, Toni and his parents would make damn sure he'd end up a humble one. Were he to be applauded for his humility, as he often has been, that too would be disdained as excessive praise. "Humble is the way you have to be, period," Toni says. "There's no special merit in it. What's more, I wouldn't use the word 'humble' to describe Rafael. He just knows his place in the world. Everybody should know their place in the world. The point is that the world is quite big enough already without you imagining that you're big too. People sometimes exaggerate this business of humility. It's a question simply of knowing who you are, where you are, and that the world will continue exactly as it is without you."

Toni's reflex to stamp out the merest suggestion of complacency or self-regard in his nephew does not make him blind to his innate qualities, or to the influence his parents have had over him. "I don't think he would have turned out badly on his own accord," he concedes. "Because of his parents, who in their own way are just as much no-nonsense people as I am, and because of the way he is. He has always been obedient, which is a sign of intelligence in a child because it shows you understand that your elders know better than you, that you respect their superior experience of the world. So I do think the raw material we were working with here was of the finest material. But I made it my mission to encourage the tendency along. When I saw his enormous potential, I thought, beyond his actual abilities as a player, what kind of a person would I like to see on the court? Someone who has personality but is not a show-off. I don't like divas, and there are plenty of them in the world of tennis. That's why I forbade him ever to throw his racket to the ground during a match; why I always insisted on the need to put on what I call 'a good face' when he was playing—calm and serious, not angry or irritated; why it was always important to be sporting and gracious to your opponent, in victory and defeat."

Respect for other people, for everyone irrespective of who they might be or what they might do, is the starting point of everything, Toni says. "What is not acceptable is that people who have had it all in life should behave coarsely with other people. No, the higher you are, the greater your duty to treat people with respect. I would have hated my nephew to have turned out any other way, to have performed tantrums on court, to have been churlish with his opponents, with the whole world watching on TV. Or, for that matter, to be impolite with the umpires or the fans. I always say, and his parents do too, that it is more important to be a good person than a good player."

Toni is enough of a good person himself to recognize that at times he might have gone "too far in the other direction" with his nephew. His harshness toward him in training was a conscious and calculated strategy. As was his unfailingly belittling response to his nephew's early competitive successes. If Rafa hit a great forehand during a match, well, there was a lot of work to do still on his backhand If he hit an impressive succession of strokes deep toward the baseline, yes, but what about his volleys? If he won a tournament, it was no big deal, and besides, what about his serve?

"You haven't achieved anything yet," Toni would say. "We need more, much more!"

The rest of the family looked on with a bemusement that, in the case of Rafa's mother, occasionally gave way to anger. His father, Sebastián, had his misgivings. His uncle Rafael wondered sometimes whether Toni was pushing his nephew too hard. His godfather, his mother's brother, Juan, went so far as to say that what Toni was doing to the child amounted to "mental cruelty."

But Toni was hard on Rafa because he knew Rafa could take it and would eventually thrive. He would not have applied the same principles, he insists, with a weaker child. The sense that perhaps he might have been right was what stopped the more doubtful members of his family from outright rebellion. One who did not doubt Toni was Miguel Ángel, the professional football player. Another disciple of the endurance principle, in which he believes with almost as much reverence as Toni himself, Miguel Ángel says that success for the elite sportsman rests on the capacity "to suffer," even to enjoy suffering.

"It means learning to accept that if you have to train two hours, you train two hours; if you have to train five, you train five; if you have to repeat an exercise fifty thousand times, you do it. That's what separates the champions from the merely talented. And it's all directly related to the winners' mentality; at the same time as you are demonstrating endurance, your head becomes stronger. The things you receive as gifts, unless they come with a special sentimental attachment, you don't value, whereas the things you achieve by your own efforts, you value a lot. The greater the effort, the greater the value." This argument prevailed in the family at least to the point that no one, not even Rafa's mother, ever really confronted Toni and told him to ease up on the child. They understood that spending so many hours and hours with Toni was wearing in the extreme, but that the two of them had reached a point where they could not live, much less succeed in tennis, without each other.

The family muttered but let Toni do his stuff, respected the sovereignty of his kingdom, a Spartan regime where no whining was allowed, where the young warrior in the making was exposed to all manner of tests and privations and was allowed no excuses, ever, however legitimate these might be. It was always his fault. If he lost a game because there happened to be a crack in the frame of his racket, Toni didn't want to know; if he played badly because the racket had not been strung tightly enough and the ball went flying, Toni remained unimpressed. If he had a temperature, if his knee hurt, if he'd had a bad day at school: nothing worked on Toni. Rafa had to grin and endure.

CHAPTER 3

THE FOOTBALL STAR
THAT NEVER WAS

FEDERER SERVED AND won the first game of the second set without losing a point. Had there been the slightest suggestion of complacency in some remote corner of my head after winning the first set, this killed it. He pounded down four good serves with that deceptively easy action of his, and I had no reply. This was most definitely not going to be a repeat of the French Open final, in which he only won four games in total and I won the last set 6-0. He was fighting hard. If he won today, it would be his sixth Wimbledon title in a row, a feat no one had ever achieved. He'd won so much, he'd been so dominant for so long, that a part of him was playing, as he had said once, "for history." Winning this match meant as much to him as it did to me; losing would be as painful for either of us.

In the second game, on my serve, he was more fired up than I remembered seeing him. Normally more serene on court than I am, he won the first two points with sensational forehands, one down the line and another cross court, to each of which he responded with a defiant yell. He won the game, broke my serve, blew me away. When Federer has these patches of utter brilliance, the only thing you can do is try and stay calm, wait for the storm to pass. There is not much you can do when the best player in history is seeing the ball as big as a football and hitting it with power, confidence, and laser accuracy. It happens and you have to be ready for it. You can't let yourself be demoralized; you have to remember— or you have to convince yourself—that he cannot possibly sustain that level of play game after game, that—as Toni feels he needs to remind me—he is human too, that if you stay cool and stick to your game plan and keep trying to wear him down and make him uncomfortable, he'll leave that zone sooner or later. His mental intensity will slacken, and you'll have your chance. This time it was going to come later rather than sooner. He won his serve again, comfortably. I just about held on to win mine, and then he won his serve again. He was 4–1 up inside what seemed like five minutes of play. My first set victory felt like a long, long way off.

But then, I had a long, long history of playing matches in which worse setbacks had been overcome. I had the experience to cope. There is nothing bigger than a Wimbledon final, but there is a limit to just how nervous you can get during a match, any match, or how important winning can be to you and, as I never forget, the tension and the euphoria are as great when you play a match as a child, when your dreams stretch no farther than the Balearic Islands junior football cup, or winning the Spanish under-12s national tennis championship. We were all very happy the evening I won that, at the age of eleven, but as usual it was Toni, unable to repress his instinct to bring me down to earth, who spoiled the party. He phoned up the Spanish Tennis Federation pretending to be a journalist and asked them for the list of the title's last twenty-five winners. Then, in front of the rest of the family, he read out the names and asked me if I had ever heard of any of them. So and so, do you know him?

No. This guy? No. And this one? No. There were just five who had reached a decent level as professionals, whose names meant something to me. Toni was triumphant. "You see? The chances of you making it as a pro are one in five. So, Rafael, don't get too excited about today's victory. There's still a long, hard road ahead. And it all depends on you."

Another thing that depended on me then was whether I was going to get sufficiently serious about my tennis to give up football. It was one of the hardest decisions I have had to confront, though in the end circumstances decided for me.

By now I was training five times a week and traveling abroad to compete in tennis tournaments, playing and winning in Europe against some of the best kids my age in the world. Yet I was still training during the week with my football team, then playing competitive games at weekends. And, as my mother reminded me, there was the matter of my school studies to attend to. Something had to give. I didn't want it to be football. The very idea broke my heart. But in the end there wasn't much choice. I knew and my parents knew that I couldn't do everything. The pain would have been greater had my football team not been taken over by a new coach. The previous coach, whom I loved, had understood that I couldn't be relied on to turn up at all our training sessions, but he was still happy for me to play for the team because I was the top goal scorer. The new guy was more dogmatic. He said that if I didn't turn up to train as all the other boys did, I couldn't play. If I missed just one training session a week, I was out of the team. So that was that. But for that coach, things might have turned out differently in my life. My father reckons that I could have gone on to become a good professional football player. He says that when I trained at football, I trained harder than all the other boys. And I did have that unusual self-confidence—or lunatic faith—in my team's ability to win games against impossible odds.

I suspect, all the same, that my father had too much faith in my talents as a footballer. I was good but not that special. Tennis was the game at which I excelled, even if I enjoyed football as much, or more. I was a part of the Balearic Islands championship team in football but under-12s champion of Spain in tennis, and finalist that same year in the under-14 national championship. I was one year younger than my teammates in the football team but often two— sometimes three—years younger than my rivals in tennis.

A choice had to be made, and there was no disputing the evidence. Tennis it had to be. I have no regrets, because it was the right choice and because I am not a person who sees any value in dwelling on things you cannot change. And I think I understood it pretty well back then too. On YouTube, you can see a video of me when I was twelve being interviewed on TV during the under-14's Spanish championships. In it, after explaining that I trained every day from four to eight in the evening, I say: "I enjoy football, but that's just for fun." I wasn't even twelve and I already had a career.

There was no letup from Toni. No mercy. At the end of training one day in Manacor when I was thirteen I had the not very bright idea of trying to jump over the net, with disastrous results. I am not naturally very well coordinated. If I have found my rhythm on the tennis court it's because I've worked at it. In my family I have a reputation for clumsiness. My godmother, Marilén, remembers how on Sunday mornings when I was a child the family would set off on bicycle rides. But I didn't like to join in. I never felt comfortable on a bike. Or on a motorbike. Both are favorite forms of transport in the eastern half of Mallorca where I live, because it is mostly flat, but I was afraid I'd fall and I never took to either. When I got my driving license, Marilén exclaimed, "What a danger for us all!" I took the point and ever since have been a cautious driver.

My godfather, Juan, says I inherited my clumsiness from my mother, who as a child always used to fall and bump into things. That's what happened to me that time after training in Manacor when I jumped the net. I tripped and fell badly, landing with my full weight on my wrist. It was a sprain and, what's more, I was bleeding. Toni had no sympathy. "You, Rafael, you have got nothing inside your head!" he said. My godfather was there at the time, and while he had always been very cautious about criticizing Toni openly, this time he could not hold back. "Toni," he said, "you've gone too far this time."

My godfather drove me to the medical center in town to get me bandaged up. He was angry. He said that my uncle had been in the wrong. He understood that Toni was hardening me up for the battles that lay ahead and all that, but he'd crossed a line now. I was in pain and didn't say anything, but one thing I understood better than my godfather was how important Toni was to me now that all my life's ambitions centered on tennis; how unwise it would be, however great the temptation at that moment, to stoke family friction around the figure of Toni or allow myself to harbor negative thoughts about him. What I wanted was to triumph at tennis, and anything that got in the way of that dream, be it spending a lazy summer with my friends or building up feelings of antagonism toward Toni, had to be put to one side.

Because Toni was right. So often infuriating but, in the long run, right. Harsh lessons such as the one that Toni taught me that day have made me more able to live with the professional athlete's burden of playing with pain. I put the lesson into practice even before I turned professional, when I won the Spanish under-14 national championships, not long after that fall at the net. That was one of the most memorable victories of my life because not only did I have to beat my opponent in the final, I had to overcome the pain barrier every inch of the way. The tournament took place in Madrid, and my rival was one of my best friends, and one of my best to this day, Toméu Salva, with whom I'd trained since the age of twelve.

In the very first round of the tournament I fell and broke the little finger of my left hand. But I refused to pull out or, under Toni's vigilant eye, to complain. I'd got to the semis the year before, and this time I intended to win. So I played right through to the end and beat Toméu in the final, beating him 6–4 in the third set. I had to grip the racket with four fingers, the broken one dangling, limp and lifeless. I didn't bandage it because that would have made it more difficult to hit the ball. The biggest difficulty was on the forehand drive. On the two-handed backhand the weight shifts more to the right hand. I played through the pain to the point that I almost forgot about it. It's a question of concentration, of putting everything out of your mind beyond the game itself. The principle has applied throughout my career. Titín's judgment, having seen me in terrible shape many times before a match but perfectly capable once play starts, is that the adrenaline of competition helps kill the pain. Whatever the explanation, I look back at that teenage Rafael and I am proud of him. He set a benchmark of endurance that has served me as an example and as a reminder ever since that you *can* put mind over matter, and if you want something badly enough, no sacrifice is too great.

The measure of what I did in that final against Toméu came after I'd won the last point. The pain hit me so hard I couldn't even lift up the cup. Another boy had to help me hold it up for the commemorative photograph.

Around that time, when I was still fourteen, I had a chance to break my ties with Toni. I was offered a scholarship to move to Barcelona, half an hour's flight away from Mallorca, to train at the High Performance Centre of San Cugat, one of the best professional tennis academies in Europe. It was another big decision for me, and the truth is, I am not very good at making decisions, even now. Split-second ones on the court, sure; decisions that need some pondering off it, not so much. (That was why I was grateful, in a way, that the new coach had appeared on the football scene a couple of years earlier to make the decision for me to renounce the game I loved and opt for tennis.) So at moments like this I listen to what other people have to say before trying to weigh up the arguments. I don't like to have opinions on things until I've got hold of all the facts. On this particular decision, it was my parents I listened to more than Toni, and they had it very clear. Given that we had a choice, being well off enough not to have to take the scholarship, my parents' view was "He is doing very well with Toni and, besides, where is a boy going to be better off than at home?" Their main fear, never mind my tennis game, was that I might lose my bearings in Barcelona, alone without the family. They did not want me to become a problem adolescent. Avoiding that was more important to them than seeing me achieve success in my tennis career.

I was glad that was the decision my parents made because, in my heart of hearts, I did not want to leave home, either, and I am gladder still today looking back on it. Grating on my nerves as Toni sometimes was (in those days he had a habit of arranging with me to meet for training at nine in the morning and not arriving till ten), I knew I had a good thing going with him. I was not going to find a better coach, or guide.

Success might have gone to my head in Barcelona; it never would with Toni or my family around, all of whom conspired to keep me grounded—Maribel, my younger sister, included. I remember a little incident involving her at a junior tournament in Tarbes, France, called *Les Petits As* (The Little Aces), when I was fourteen. It's considered to be the world championship for kids of that age. The crowds are big, people believing they will get a first look at some of the stars of the future. I won that year, and in my first taste of what was to come, girls my age or older started coming up to me to ask for my signature. My parents, seeing this, were amused but also slightly alarmed. So my father got Maribel, who was nine, to join the queue of girls and, when she reached me, to ask me in the most fawning, sickly sweet way, "Mr. Nadal, please can I have your autograph?" My parents, watching from a distance, laughed approvingly. Others might have been terribly impressed by me, but never my family.

That same year I went on a trip to South Africa, the farthest by far I'd ever been from home. After winning a series of tournaments in Spain sponsored by Nike, I qualified to go to a grand final in South Africa, the Nike Junior Tour International, where the winners of all the other countries gathered to compete. Toni wasn't too sure I should go. As usual, he didn't want me to get ideas above myself. But, in terms of preparing me for the wandering life of a professional tennis player, he did see the merits of me playing in a distant land against some of the best foreign players my age. While Toni hemmed and hawed (he has strong opinions on things but struggles to make decisions even more than I do), my father had no doubts. He phoned another coach I sometimes worked with in Palma, Jofre

Porta, and asked him if he'd go with me to South Africa. Jofre said yes, and that same evening we set off, via Madrid, on an overnight flight to Johannesburg. Toni gave the impression of not being too pleased, but a part of him would have been relieved, given that he has a phobia of planes, to have been saved twelve hours in the air.

I remember that tournament less as a tennis player than as an excited child on his first trip to Africa. It was played in Sun City, an amazingly extravagant complex in the heart of the African bush, where there were giant swimming pools and cascades and even an artificial beach and, nearby, lions and elephants. It was a thrill to be near these wild animals—but not too near. We were taken to a place where we could hold and stroke some white lion pups, but I didn't touch one myself. I'm not comfortable with animals, not even with dogs. I doubt their intentions. But I remember South Africa as a thrilling trip, in which I also happened to win a tennis tournament. Evidence of how childlike I remained, how unprofessional still for all the hours of hard practice I put in, and for all Toni's cajoling, was provided on the morning of the final, two hours of which I spent playing football. The organizers were scandalized, as if their tournament was not being taken seriously enough, and they appealed to Jofre to stop me playing. He didn't. Knowing he was reflecting the views of my parents, he reminded them that if traveling halfway across the world to play in a tournament wasn't fun, the point would come when I'd lose my enthusiasm for tennis.

I found out after my return home from South Africa that my godmother had arranged a party at my grandparents' to celebrate my victory. She'd even hung up a banner. But I never got to see it. Toni, having got wind of what was afoot, snatched the banner angrily off the wall, and took it away. Even though the words my godmother had written on the banner were intended in a jokey, almost teasing spirit—celebrating and deflating at the same time—Toni didn't see the funny side of it at all. He intercepted me at the door of my grandparents' home and said to me, "You can go home now. I'll come along after I've given your godmother and grandparents a talking to." I don't know exactly what he said to them, but the gist of it, as my godmother reported later, was this: "Are you crazy? What are you trying to do to Rafael? You'll ruin him. Don't give what he does so much importance!"

Toni did not stop there. He came round to my house later that night and said, "OK, we can't waste time. I'll meet you downstairs at nine tomorrow and we'll drive to Palma for training." Flabbergasted, stunned into rebellion, I replied: "Toni, do you understand what you're asking me to do?" And he replied, "What am I asking? Simply that you be downstairs at nine ready to train. I'll wait for you. Don't make me come upstairs." I was indignant, that familiar feeling again that I was being treated unjustly. "Are you serious? If so, you're nuts. Do you think it's fair," I continued, "that after a flight of fourteen or fifteen hours you shouldn't let me off one, just one, training session?" He said, "I'll see you at nine, then." I replied, "Well, I won't be there." But I was there. Unhappy, grumpy, in a filthy mood, at nine o'clock sharp.

He was right, and, for all my outrage, I knew deep down he was right too. Once more, his purpose had been to avoid any prospect of me "believing" my successes, thinking they were worthy either of celebration or special dispensations from training. My parents are more festive than Toni, not such party poopers, but on this occasion they agreed with his approach. My mother's reaction when an uncle or an aunt congratulated me on a victory was invariably the same: "Come on. It's not such a big deal."

My mother put her energy and encouragement into the areas

where I was less strong, such as my school studies. It was on this account that my parents, having shielded me from Barcelona, decided when I turned fifteen that I should do as my father, and Toni, had done and go to a boarding school in Palma. Called the Balearic Sports School, it was tailored to my needs—regular school lessons but plenty of tennis built in—and it was only an hour's drive from home. But I was miserable there. My parents—my mother in particular—were concerned that all this tennis was killing my studies. My concern was that the studies were going to kill my tennis. They killed my chances of playing at the Wimbledon Junior Tournament and the one at Roland Garros too. "But these tournaments are so important!" I complained to my mother. To which she replied, "Yes, I'm certain of it, but I assure you that you'll have another chance to play in those competitions; but if you abandon your studies, you most definitely will not have another chance to pass your exams."

The sports boarding school seemed to my parents to be the best bet for me to accomplish both goals. I don't want to say it was a big mistake on their part, because I did pass my exams. But it turned out to be a terrible year. I didn't need or want anything to change in my life. I was happy with what I had. And suddenly I was terribly homesick, missing my parents, my sister, the family meals with my uncles and grandparents, the football games on TV at night—missing those, that was a killer—and home food. And the timetable was brutal. We got up at seven thirty, had classes from eight to eleven, then tennis for two and a half hours, then we ate. Then it was classes again from three to six in the evening, and from six to eight tennis and physical training. And then from nine to eleven at night we had to study again. It was too much. I wasn't doing either thing I had to do well, my studies or my tennis. The only good thing I remember of that experience was that I was so exhausted at the end of the day that I slept well. The other saving grace was that I went home for weekends and that, yes, I got the qualifications I needed to bring my schooling to a satisfactory end.

My mother wanted me to carry on studying and take the exams necessary to get into university. So she signed me up when I was sixteen to a long distance course, but I lost all my books, left them on a plane on a flight to the Canary Islands, and that was the end of my formal education. I don't think I left those books behind deliberately; it was just another case of me being absentminded in all things other than tennis. And I don't regret having given up the chance to go to university, because I don't have regrets, period. I'm curious about the world; I like to inform myself about what's going on, and I think I've learned more than enough things about life in recent years that university could never teach.

The funny thing is that at boarding school I followed in the footsteps of Toni, who also missed home terribly. My father, on the other hand, never felt that way. He has always played the cards that life deals him. I don't have the overall solidity of character that he has, nor does Toni, but I do apply the endurance principle in my tennis. Toni provided the theory, my father the practice; Toni taught me to endure, my father gave me an example to imitate.

His personality is the polar opposite of Toni's. Toni is a big talker, a philosopher; my father is a listener and a pragmatist. Toni has opinions, my father makes decisions, always with a clear head. Toni is unpredictable; my father is even-tempered. Toni can be unfair; my father is just. And he is the doer in the family. Toni's project has been me, and he's done his job impeccably. But my father, two years older than Toni, has started one business after another from scratch;

he's single-minded about his objectives, but he's made his family his first responsibility. He's very honest, jealous not to dishonor the family name. He's employed dozens of people in his various businesses and created the conditions for us to live well and for Toni to dedicate himself to me.

One thing would not have happened without the other. Toni has never received any money from me or from anyone in the family for the lifelong attention he's dedicated to me, but he's been able to do it because he owns half of my father's business, and takes half the profits, without doing any of the work. It's been a fair exchange because I would never have had anything like the same hours of coaching from Toni if my father had not worked with such purpose all his life.

What defines my father in his work is that he faces problems, finds solutions, gets the job done. And there I think is where I take after him, more than after Toni. Toni is my tennis coach and my life coach too. His medium is words: he urges me on, berates me, gives me advice, teaches me. But that is where his work ends and mine begins. The one who has to put his words into action is me. My godmother says my father is by nature a winner and that on court I have his character. I think that's true. I'm the fighter in my ring, as my father is in his.

Yet, in terms of the public, he is the one in the shadows. As he enjoys saying, "I've been the son of Rafael Nadal, the brother of Miguel Ángel Nadal, the father of Rafael Nadal—never myself, alone." Others might respond to this circumstance with envy, or barely concealed bitterness. My father genuinely delights in it. His father was a celebrity in Manacor because of his musical prowess; his brother was a celebrated football player; his son is a celebrated tennis player. This has meant that my father, at different stages of his life, had to introduce himself, or be introduced, as the son/ brother/father of another Nadal. Or if he says, "Hello, I'm Sebastián Nadal," the response has invariably been "Oh, the son/brother/ father of . . . ?" Ever since my father can remember there's been at least one item a week in the local media about a Nadal, but never about him. But it's never bothered him, because he genuinely has no interest in being known or recognized, much less feted. He is happy simply for it to be understood by the rest of us that he has tried to be a pillar for the family and, in recent years, for me in particular.

It was my father the businessman who understood early on in my career that we should create a professional team around me. In addition to Toni, we hooked up with Joan Forcades, my physical trainer; Rafael "Titín" Maymó, my physical therapist; Ángel Cotorro, my doctor; Benito Pérez Barbadillo to deal with media communications; and as my agent, Carlos Costa, who works for IMG, a sports marketing company very well plugged into the tennis world. On business matters related to my tennis career, my father said that, contrary to his usual instincts, he thought it wise for us to receive input from people outside the family. I told him I trusted him entirely but if he felt more comfortable working with people who might add a more objective point of view, that was fine by me. So he teamed up with some tried and trusted associates that he has worked with, and who I myself have known since I was a child. The truth is, though, that the business aspect of things is not something I worry about very much. Toni, always the conservative, wasn't keen on expanding things beyond the small family nucleus, but it was my father who said, no, if we are going to aim for the top, we have to recognize our limitations and get some good pros to work with us. My father is the strategic brain of our team but he is not above taking care of minor matters too, when others are not available to help, such as finding a couple of Wimbledon tickets for a sponsor or sorting out transportation from a hotel to a club where a tournament is taking place. With big things and little things that arise, it's my dad who brings the order and calm and good humor that I need to function at peak focus on the tennis court.

This is not to diminish in any way the role Toni has played in my life. For all the clashes we've had, he's my uncle and I love him. But the principal driving force in my life has been my father, who, along with my mother, created a happy and stable home base without which I would not be the tennis player I am. Maybe it was not the best thing for her, but she practically abandoned her own self—leaving behind a perfume shop she owned—and sacrificed everything for us, for my sister, my father, and me. She is a social person by nature, who loves to learn and see new things, but her life became confined to the family after I was born. She did it because she wanted to, because she never had any doubts this was what she had to do. I sometimes think she made too many personal sacrifices for us. But if her objective was that we should have the space and love necessary to thrive, it worked. While my father was out managing his businesses, she was the one who shaped our values, who took charge of my education and my sister's, who helped us with our homework, who fed us and was with us every day, always available to us for anything. To underestimate the value of her role in everything that has come my way, to see her importance as less than Toni's, for example, would be as blind as it would be unjust. As she sometimes says, "Would you like to see written all over the place that someone else raised your child?"

Yet, as I tell my mother, it suits me right now to have him occupying a central role in my tennis life. It is in my best interests. He gives me something without which my game would suffer. And I think that my mother, reluctantly at times, understands that.

I can never repay my parents for what they have given me, but the best thing I can do for them is try and remain faithful to the values they've instilled in me, try to be "good people," because I know that nothing would hurt them more or make them feel more betrayed than if I were not. If, in addition, I can give them the fun and joy and satisfaction of winning a big tournament, like Wimbledon, that is a thrilling bonus. Because a victory for me is a victory for all of us. I know it and they do too.

That thought would not have been uppermost in my mind after going 4–1 down to Federer in the second set of the final at Wimbledon, but if I had the conviction that this was a mountain I could still climb, a lot of it had to do with the stability my family had given me and the example they had set.

Nonetheless, the situation was far from ideal. Here I was before the Wimbledon champion of champions, and Federer was playing tennis as well as he ever had. I was being outplayed. From the outside it must have looked as if Federer was suddenly looking majestically comfortable in his Centre Court kingdom. An observer might have imagined I was thinking, "Oh my God! I'm letting this slip. It's going to be 2007 all over again." But no. I was thinking, "He cannot sustain this level either in this set or the next three or four sets. I still feel good. The sensations are there. Just stick to your game plan and you'll be back." And never, ever give up a point.

And I started to win. Sooner than I expected or, for that matter, entirely deserved. I won my serve and was then lucky to break his. That was a setback for him. He took it badly, lost his concentration, left that zone of brilliance he had entered, and I broke him again. He was hitting loose shots, usually due to finding himself in awkward positions after trying to twist around the barrage of balls I kept aiming at his backhand, gifting me points where before he was winning them with seeming ease. He was beginning to feel uncomfortable again, to feel the pressure, and his face showed it. He shouted too, a couple of times, in furious irritation. This was not Roger's style at all. But at that point I was cooler outside than he was, and probably inside too. Not that I had really upped my own game. I played some poor shots myself, missed some winners I should have put away fairly simply. I'm not poker-faced at these moments. I do let out yelps of frustration, or close my eyes in despair, as anybody who has watched me play knows. But as soon as I take up my position for the next point, the frustration is gone, forgotten, erased, and what counts, all that exists, is the moment.

I was 5–4 up and serving. He won the first point, then I hit a good first serve straight to his body, to which he had no answer. Fifteen all. Then I won the next point with a drive deep on his forehead corner, very similar to the shot with which I had won the first point of the match. But he came back and it was thirty all. A big point. And then, as I was bouncing the ball up and down on the grass, just about to wind up my body to serve, the umpire cut in. "Time violation: warning, Mr. Nadal." I had apparently spent too long between points, gone over the legal limit of twenty seconds before I served—a rule that is enforced only rarely. But it's a dangerous rule. Because once you've received that first warning, any subsequent violations lead to the deduction of points. My concentration had been put to the test. I could have made a scene. The crowd, I could tell, shared my indignation. But I knew, without having to give it a second thought, that to let my feelings show would do me no good. I'd risk losing that precious asset, my concentration. Besides, the momentum was with me and I was two points away from winning the second set. I put the umpire's interruption immediately out of my mind and won the point with a terrific and, for me, very unusual shot. A backhand slice, cross-court, that defeated his lunge at the net. That was especially satisfying. Not just because of the importance of the point but because I like to believe that, however many tournaments I win, I keep improving my game, and the backhand slice was an element of my game I'd been working on strengthening for some time. It's not a shot all that many players choose to have in their repertoire because the game is so relentlessly fast nowadays, but I believe it gives me an edge, another option, allowing me to change the rhythm of the game, ask new questions of my opponent. But this particular shot exceeded all my expectations. Normally the sliced backhand is a defensive shot; the one I had just pulled out of the hat had been one of the best winners of my life. And it gave me set point. He came right back, leveling the score at deuce, but I was feeling at the top of my game now, capable of anything. The game did go to two more deuces and he had three break points in all, but finally he surrendered the game and the set with a hesitant backhand into the net. It was an unforced error, at a decisive moment, in a match that would be marked by an extraordinarily high percentage of winners. I was up 6–4, 6–4. One more set and I'd be Wimbledon champion.

But I wasn't smelling victory. Not at all. This was Federer, and against him there was no relaxation possible. What was more, I knew that the 6–4 score had been unjust. He had played better than me overall in the set. He could play at the same level, or not as well, and win the next one. I might have beaten him mentally; but he'd beat me if I mentally let up. I looked up and saw the sky darkening. It looked like rain. The match might have to be postponed till Monday. Whatever came, I'd deal with it. The scoreboard said I was two sets to love up; but in my mind it was still 0–0.

THE CLAN

SEBASTIÁN NADAL CAME in for much teasing from his family over the jacket he wore to watch his son play Federer in the 2008 Wimbledon final. It wasn't his jacket, he complained; he didn't have one before the match began, he asked Benito Pérez, his son's press chief, to see if he could come up with something, and the best Benito was able to come up with was a dark blue jacket with vertical silver stripes that, along with the dark sunglasses, made him look, somewhat discordantly in the strawberries-and-cream setting of the Centre Court, like a third-rate Sicilian mafia boss. That was how his brothers described him, at any rate, and it was an impression the justice of which he himself struggled to dispute.

There was a sense in which the gangster look was not entirely inappropriate. There is something Sicilian about the closeness of the Nadal family circle. They live on a Mediterranean island, and more than a family, they are a clan—the Corleones, or the Sopranos, without the malice, or the guns. They communicate in a dialect only the islanders speak; they are blindly loyal to one another, and they conduct all business within the family, be it the terms of Miguel Ángel's contract with Barcelona Football Club, the glass enterprise

Sebastián runs, or the real estate deals in which they have all prof-itably dabbled.

Take the five-storey building the family bought in the very heart of Manacor, next to the ancient church of Our Lady of Dolours whose tall spire dominates the town's skyline. When Rafael was between ten and twenty-one years old, all the Nadals—the grand-parents, the four brothers, and the sister, plus their spouses and their gradually mushrooming offspring—lived in the same apartment block, one on top of the other, the front doors often open by day and by night, converting the building into one great big family mansion.

In Porto Cristo, the seaside resort eight kilometers away from Manacor, they had a similar setup. On the ground floor, the grand-parents; on the first floor, Sebastián's family; on the second, Nadal's godmother, Marilén; on the third, Uncle Rafael. Then, across the road, Toni, and a little way down the street, Miguel Ángel.

Rafa's grandparents were the masterminds behind an arrange-ment that is not entirely unusual in a society as intensely familial as Mallorca, where it is still not unusual for sons and daughters to remain living with their parents well into their thirties.

"Keeping everybody together was a task that my wife and I set ourselves," says Don Rafael Nadal, the musical grandfather. "We did not have to struggle too hard to convince my children to make the effort to acquire the building. I've mentally conditioned them all since they were very small to keep everything inside the family."

That was why, when Miguel Ángel signed up as a professional footballer, there was no question of anyone other than his big brother Sebastián acting as his agent, and doing so for free. It would not have occurred to Sebastián to ask for a cut of his brother's winnings. If you live by the Nadal family code, Sebastián explained, you just don't do that. What three of the brothers—Sebastián, Miguel Ángel,

Toni—and Rafa have done is set up a company called Nadal Invest that has put money into real estate. As far as Rafa's multiple sponsorship deals with Spanish and international companies, initially Sebastián oversaw them himself, principally the first deals with Nike. The person on whom the important decisions ultimately rest is Sebastián, who has taken over where his own father, Don Rafael, left off as family patriarch: definer of the values, keeper of the rules.

"I'd lose anything, I'd give up anything—money, property, cars, anything—rather than fight with my family," Sebastián says. "It is inconceivable for us to have a bust-up. We never have and we never will. Seriously. No joke. Family loyalty is our first and last rule. It comes before anything. My best and closest friends are my family, then come the rest. Family unity is the pillar of our lives."

It is, because the principle is taken to such extremes that they shun what would otherwise be the entirely natural impulse to congratulate Rafa when he wins. Marilén, the godmother, did try it once, and immediately Toni and Rafa's response was to look at her incredulously and say, "*What* are you doing?" "They were right," Marilén says. "It was as if I were congratulating myself. Because if one of us wins, we all win."

CHAPTER 4

HUMMINGBIRD

EASING UP WAS not an option. Two sets to love up and one set away from winning Wimbledon, people watching might have felt I was within easy reach of my life's dream. But I intended to allow no such thoughts into my head. I would take each point as it came, in isolation. I'd forget everything else, obliterate the future and the past, exist only in the moment.

Federer winning the first game of the set to love, serving and firing winning drives with the purpose of a man who was not remotely ready to give up the battle, if anything, actually helped my concentration, reminded me that being ahead meant nothing; winning over the long haul was all. I began preparing myself for what suddenly seemed like it might be a very long haul indeed. Partly because the sky was darkening again, threatening rain, but mainly because Federer continued playing the way he had begun, making a high percentage of winners, holding his serve easily, forcing break point after break point on mine, making me battle hard to stop him running away with the set.

People ask me sometimes whether I feel I've spoiled Federer's party, whether my appearance on the tennis scene might have prevented him from setting more records. To which my answer is "How about looking at it another way? How about it's me whose party *he's* spoiled?" Had he not been around, maybe I could have been world number one four years in a row by 2008, instead of watching and waiting all that time as number two. The truth probably is that had one of us not been around, the other would have triumphed more. But it's also true that the rivalry has benefitted us both in terms of our international profiles—among other things resulting in more interest from sponsors—because it's made the game of tennis more appealing to more people. When it's a procession, as we say in Spain, when one player wins time after time, it's good for the player but not necessarily good for the game. And I think that, in the end, what is good for the game has to be good for the two of us. There's an excitement generated among the fans when we are about to meet, usually in finals because of our number one and two seedings, that touches us too. We've played so many games against each other, so many of them incredibly close and exciting, and crucial in our careers, because often they've been Grand Slam finals. If I've had an edge in matches won—and I led by 11–6 before the Wimbledon 2008 final—it's because we've played a number of our matches on clay, where I do have the upper hand; but if you look at the other surfaces we've played on, you'll see that the results are more even.

All this is not to say that there aren't plenty of other good players out there more than capable of beating us both, and who do beat us both. I'm thinking of Djokovic—especially Djokovic—but also Murray, Soderling, Del Potro, Berdych, Verdasco, David Ferrer, Davydenko . . . But the record since I became number two in 2006 shows that Federer and I have dominated the big tournaments, playing against each other in many of the big finals. This has meant, and I think we both sense it, that our rivalry has been acquiring an ever-greater magic in people's minds. The expectation our matches generate brings out the best in me. Whenever I play against Federer, I have the feeling that I have to play at the very limit of my capacities, that I have to be perfect, and that I have to stay perfect for a long time in order to win. As for him, I think he attacks more against me, plays more aggressively, goes for winners on his drives and volleys more than he does with other players, obliging him to take more risks and to be at 100 percent in order to win.

Whether he's made me a better player, or I him, it's hard for me to say. Toni has never ceased to remind me—and I know he is right—that Federer is more technically gifted than I am, but he does so not to cause me despondency, but because he knows saying so will motivate me to sharpen my game. I watch Federer playing on video sometimes, and I'll be amazed at how good he is; surprised that I have been able to beat him. Toni and I watch a lot of tennis videos, especially of my games, both ones that I've won and ones that I've lost. Everybody tries to take lessons from defeat, but I try to take them from my victories too. You have to remember that often in tennis you win by only the finest of margins, that there is an element of mathematical unfairness built into the game. It's not like basketball, where the winner is always the one who has accumulated the most points. In tennis the outcome often turns less on being the better player overall than on winning points at critical times. That's why tennis is such a psychological sport. It's also a reason why you should never allow victory to go to your head. At the moment of triumph, yes, drink in the euphoria. But later on, when you watch a match you've won, you often realize—sometimes with a shudder— how very close you came to losing. And then you have to analyze why: was it because I lost concentration or was it because there are facets of my game I have to improve, or both?

Another thing about watching my matches again closely, dispassionately, is that in appreciating and respecting the skill of my opponents, watching them hit wonderful winners, I learn to accept losing points against them with more serene resignation. Some players rage and despair when they are aced, or when they are the victims of a magnificent passing shot. That is the path to self-destruction. And it is crazy, because it means you believe yourself to be capable, in some kind of ideal tennis world, of subduing your opponent's game from start to finish. If you give your opponent more credit, if you accept that he played a shot you could do nothing about, if you play the part of the spectator for a moment and generously acknowledge a magnificent piece of play, there you win balance and inner calm. You take the pressure off yourself. In your head, you applaud; visibly, you shrug; and you move on to the next point, aware not that the tennis gods are ranged against you or that you are having a miserable day, but that there is every possibility next time that it will be you who hits the unplayable winner.

In the end, you have to understand that the difference in ability between the top players is marginal, practically nothing, and that the matches between us are decided in a handful of points. When I say, and when Toni says, that a large part of the reason why I have been successful is my humility, I don't mean it in a sappy, PR-savvy sort of way, or because I am trying to make out that I am a well-balanced, morally superior sort of individual. Understanding the importance of humility is to understand the importance of being in a state of maximum concentration at the crucial stages of a game, knowing that you are not going to go out and win on God-given talent alone. I am not very comfortable talking about myself in comparison to other players, but I do think that maybe in the mental department I have developed something of an edge. That is not to say that I am not afraid, that I don't have my doubts as to how things will go at the start of each year. I do—precisely because I know that there is so little difference between one player and another. But I do think I have a capacity to accept difficulties and overcome them that is superior to many of my rivals'.

Maybe that is why I like golf so much, because it's a game that also plays to the discipline I've acquired in tennis to stay calm under pressure. You need a base of talent, obviously, and lots of practice, but what's decisive in golf is not letting one bad shot affect the rest of your game. If there is one sportsman that I admire outside the game of tennis, it is Tiger Woods. When he is at his best, I see in him what I would like to be myself. I like that winning look he has when he plays, and I like most of all his attitude, his way of facing up to the moments of crisis when a game is won or lost. He might hit a bad shot and get angry with himself, but the next time he squares up to hit the ball, he is back in focus. He almost always does what he has to do when the pressure is on, he almost never makes the wrong decision. Evidence of that is the fact that he has never lost a tournament when he has gone out at the top of the leader board in the last round. To be able to do that you have to be very good, but that alone is not enough. You have to be able to judge when to take a risk and when to hold back; you have to be able to accept your mistakes, seize the opportunities that come your way, when to opt for one type of shot, when for another. I've never had an idol in any sport, not even in football. When I was a child, I did have a special admiration for my fellow Mallorcan Carlos Moyá, but never the blind admiration of the doting fan. It's not in my nature, in my culture, or in the way I've been brought up. But the closest I have come to an idol is definitely Tiger Woods. It's not his swing, so much, or even the way he strikes the ball. It's his clearheadedness, his determination, his attitude. I love it.

He is an example and an inspiration for me in my tennis game, and my golf game too. Excessively so in golf, according to my friends, who think I take the game way too seriously. The difference is that they play for fun and I find it impossible to play any game without giving 100 percent. This means that when I go out on the golf course with my friends, as when I go out on court to face Federer, everyday human feelings are put on hold. I have a phrase I use before a game to set the boundary between our enmity on the course and our affection off it. I look hard at my golfing pals and say, "Hostile match, right?" I know they laugh at me behind my back about this, but I am not going to change. I am decidedly unfriendly during a golf game, from the first hole to the last.

It's true that you don't need the same intensity of concentration as in tennis, where, if your mind wanders for three or four minutes, you can lose three or four games. In golf you have more than three or four minutes between shots. In tennis you have a split second to decide whether to go for a winning drive, a defensive slice, or rush to the net for a volley. In golf you can take thirty seconds over the ball, if you wish, to prepare yourself for a shot. Which means there's plenty of time to joke and chat about other things during a round. But that's not the way I play the game, even with my uncles, even with my friend Toméu Salva, much less with my sister's boyfriend, who is a scratch player. I take my cue from Tiger Woods. From start to finish, I barely say a word to my rivals; I certainly don't compliment them on a good shot. They complain, they get angry with me, curse me for my rudeness. They say I'm more aggressive even than I am on the tennis court, that on court I've been known to smile, but on the golf course I never do, until the game is over. The difference between me and my friends, some of whom are much better golfers than I am (I have a handicap of 11), is that I just don't see the point of playing a sport unless you're giving it your all.

The same goes for training, which has caused me problems sometimes when the players I've chosen for practice during tournaments say that I train too hard, too soon, that I don't give them a chance to warm up and they are tired out in ten minutes. It's been a common complaint all along my career. But I haven't sold my soul to tennis. The effort I invest is great, but I don't consider it a sacrifice. It's true that I've trained every day practically since the age of six and that I make big demands of myself. And meanwhile my friends are out partying or sleeping late. But I haven't felt this to be a sacrifice or a loss because I've always enjoyed it. That is not to say that there haven't been times when I'd have liked to do something else—such as stay in bed after a late night out instead of training. As I say, though, I do have late nights. Very late nights, as is the way in Mallorca, especially in summer. I barely touch alcohol, but I do go out dancing with my friends and sometimes stay up till six in the morning. I might have missed out on some things other young men have, but I felt, on balance, that I've made a good trade-off.

Some players are monks, but I'm not. That's not my understanding of how to live life. Tennis is my passion, but I also think of it as my work, as a job that I try to do as honestly and well as if I were working in my father's glass business or in my grandfather's furniture store. And, like any job, however large the financial rewards might be, there's a lot of grind. Of course, I am incredibly fortunate to be one of those few people in the world who has a job that he enjoys, and who on top of that is paid extraordinarily well for what he does. I never, ever lose sight of that. But it does remain, in the end, work. That's how I conceive of it. Otherwise, I wouldn't train as hard as I do, with the same seriousness, intensity, and concentration as when I am playing a match. Training is not fun. When my family or friends come along to watch me practicing with Toni or with a fellow professional they know, I am in no mood for jokes or smiles; they know to keep quiet, as quiet as the Wimbledon crowds when I am playing a practice point.

But I also need to switch off and have a good time and party till late or play football with my cousins, all of whom are younger than me, or go fishing, the perfect antidote to the all action stress of tennis. My friends back home mean the world to me and not to go out with them at night to our favorite bars in Manacor and Porto Cristo would mean losing, or at any rate diluting, those friendships. And that would be no good, because if you are happy and have a good time, that also has a positive impact on your tennis, on your training and the matches you play. To deny yourself necessary pleasures would be counterproductive. You'd end up feeling bitter, hating training, and even hating tennis, or becoming bored by it, which I know has happened to players who've taken the principle of professional self-denial too far. It is possible to do everything, I believe, but always keeping a balance, never, ever losing track of what's important. In exceptional circumstances I might even skip morning training and train in the afternoon instead. What you can't do is make the exception the rule. You can train once in the afternoon, but not three afternoons running. Because then training becomes secondary in your mind, it ceases to be the priority, and that's the beginning of the end. You might as well prepare for retirement. The condition of having fun is keeping the line, sticking to your training regime: that is non-negotiable.

That said, I don't train now as much as I used to when I was fifteen or sixteen. Then I'd train four and a half, five hours a day,
partly with Toni but also a lot of the time with my physical trainer,
Joan Forcades. Forcades, another Mallorcan, does not correspond to
the image of the muscle-bound, shaven-headed, sergeant major one
sometimes has in mind when thinking of a person in his profession.
Born, like Toni, in 1960, he is a cultured man, a fanatical reader and
film buff, who thinks a hundred thoughts a minute and wears his
long hair in a ponytail. He has read every academic treatise there is
on his subject and tailored a program for me specifically designed
to strengthen every aspect of my tennis. When he worked on building up my muscular strength in those teenage years (we started
together when I was fourteen) it was not with a view to give me
a bodybuilder's physique or to shape me for the demands of track
athletics. To train as a sprinter or distance runner does not work
with tennis, because it's not what Forcades calls a "linear" game.
Tennis is an intermittent game, requiring the body to sustain an on-
off explosiveness, sprinting and braking, over a long period of time.
Forcades says a tennis player must take his example from the hum-
mingbird, the only animal that combines endless stamina with high
speed, able to manage up to eighty wing flaps per second over a
period of four hours. So we didn't build bulk for bulk's sake. To do
so would be counterproductive because in tennis what you want is
a balance between strength and speed; disproportionate muscular
weight would slow you down. Forcades would feed me the theory in
our frequent drives together from my home to a gym he had on the
coast. The training we did was infinitely varied, though when I was
sixteen, seventeen we spent a lot of time on a pulley device created
to help astronauts stop their muscles from atrophying in the weight-
lessness of space. By pulling on a cord attached to a metallic fly-

wheel I built up my arm and leg muscles, but especially my arms, so as to increase their acceleration speed, a major reason why (they tell me scientific studies have been made of this) I am able to apply more revolutions to the ball on my topspin forehands than any other player on the circuit. Training on this "YoYo" flywheel apparatus, as it's called, I reached a point where I was able to perform the equivalent of 117-kilogram lifts without using weights. I also built up my body strength in those days hoisting myself up and down by the arms on parallel bars. We did exercises in water, we used step machines and indoor rowing machines, we did some yoga, we worked on the muscles but also on the joints and a lot on the tendons, too, to prevent injuries and to improve my elasticity of movement. As for running, we would do sequences that developed my ability to change direction fast, to move sideways back and forth at speed. Everything we did simulated the special stresses tennis exacts on the body and conditioned me to adapt the best I could for the urgent, stop-start nature of the game. And there was another thing Forcades was emphatic about: that we should stick to the training regime even when I least felt like it, when I was tired or in a bad mood or, for whatever reason, just not feeling up to it. Because there would be days during a tournament when I would not be feeling at my best either and by training in such circumstances I'd be better prepared to compete when I was below par.

I trained as an adolescent the way I have continued to train: as hard as I do when I play. If ever I needed pushing, Forcades had his methods. Appealing to my competitiveness, he would say something like, "Do you know Carlos Moyá (whom he also trained) can do ten of those in thirty seconds? Well, since you're a bit tired today let's stop at eight." And then, of course, I'd do twelve.

My father and my uncles are all big, strong men, so there was nothing freakish about me developing a big, athletic body, but because I'd advanced so fast up the tennis ladder I had to make a special effort in my teens to build up my strength in order to compete with grown-up professional players. Several years passed before I found myself regularly playing against people my own age, or younger.

My first victory as a top-level professional, in an ATP tournament, came two months short of my sixteenth birthday in the Mallorca Open, against Ramón Delgado, who was ten years older than me. Thanks to this win I stepped up to the international Futures tour, the level below the ATP tour, where I won six tournaments in a row. That led me on to take part in the Challenger series, where players ranked between 100 and 300 in the world typically compete. Now I was coming up all the time against players who were twenty, twenty-two, twenty-four years old. I ended the year 2002, age sixteen and a half, ranked 199 in the world. Early in 2003, less than a year after my breakthrough win against Delgado, I played in two of the top ATP World Tour competitions, Monte Carlo and Hamburg. In the first I achieved an even bigger breakthrough than my victory over Delgado: I beat Albert Costa, who had won the French Open in 2002; and, in the second, my friend and mentor Carlos Moyá. Both were in the world top ten at the time, both of them Grand Slam tournament winners. In four months I climbed from 199 to 109 in the world rankings. I had a badly timed setback, a shoulder injury in training that took two weeks to cure and stopped me from making my debut at the French Open in Roland Garros, but shortly thereafter I played Wimbledon for the first time, making it to the third round. The ATP voted me 2003's "Newcomer of the Year." I was a teenager in a hurry, madly hyperactive, operating at a thousand revolutions a minute in training as in competition.

In 2004 my body said, "Enough!" My run was cut abruptly short by a tiny crack in a bone of my left foot that kept me out of the game from mid-April to the end of July. That meant no Roland Garros, no Wimbledon. I'd charged up to 35 in the rankings, and getting back, recovering my rhythm after such a break—the first break in my career because of injury, the first of several, as it would turn out— was not easy. At the time it was cruelly disappointing; in the long run, maybe it was no bad thing. Because the frailty of the body, in my case, has made the mind stronger. And maybe my mind needed a rest too. The wisdom and support of my family and the way Toni had programmed me to endure adversity led me not to despair but to a point where my desire to win, and my determination to do everything it would take to win, became even more clearly honed.

That period allowed me to absorb a lesson that all elite sportsmen and -women need to heed: that we are enormously privileged and fortunate, but that the price of our privilege and good fortune is that our careers end at an unnaturally young age. And, worse, that injury can cut your progress short at any time; that from one week to the next you might be forced into premature retirement. That means, first, that you must enjoy what you do; and, second, that the chances that come your way once won't necessarily come your way again, so you squeeze the most you possibly can out of every opportunity every single time, as if it were your last. Toni had conveyed that message to me in words; now, as I recovered impatiently from my injury, I felt it in my flesh and blood. The more the years pass by, the more loudly you hear the clock ticking. I know that if I manage to keep playing at the top level at the age of twenty-nine or thirty, I'll be a very lucky and very happy man. That first serious injury I had made me aware at an early age how quickly time passes for a professional athlete. It has served me in good stead. As my friend Tomeú Salva says, very quickly I became "an old young player." I attach a huge value to what I have and I try to act on that understanding in every point I play.

Not that it always works. Barely a month after my return from injury in 2004 I found myself up against Andy Roddick in the second round of the US Open in New York. Roddick, who'd won the US Open the year before, is a broad-shouldered, good guy, and he was a bit too broad-shouldered and good for me on that day. I fell abruptly to earth, obliging me to remember that, for all my successes, I was still a growing boy. Much bulkier than me in those days, Roddick was world number two then, behind Federer, having been number one the year before. I was playing him on the fast courts at Flushing Meadow, a surface I was still some way from getting to grips with. I had no answer to his enormous serve and received a sound beating, worse even than the score of 6–0, 6–3, 6–4 suggested.

But my chance would come to avenge that defeat later that year.

The highlight of 2004 was representing my country in the Davis Cup, the tennis equivalent of football's World Cup. I made my debut against the Czech Republic, when I was still seventeen, and immediately I fell in love with the competition. First, because I am proudly Spanish, which is not as trite as it sounds, because Spain is a country where a lot of people are ambiguous about their national identity and feel that their first loyalty is to their region. Mallorca is my home and always will be—I doubt very much I'll ever leave—but Spain is my country. My father feels exactly the same way, evidence of which is supplied by the fact that we're both passionate fans of Real Madrid, the Spanish capital's big club. The other reason I love the Davis Cup is that it gives me the chance to recover that sense of team belonging that I lost, with a lot of regret, when I abandoned football for tennis at the age of twelve. I'm a gregarious person, I need people around me, so it's a peculiar thing that destiny— largely in the shape of my uncle Toni—should have made me opt for a career in a game that's so solitary. Here was my chance to share once again in the collective excitement I had felt on that unforgettable day of my childhood when our football team won the championship of the Balearic Islands.

I didn't have the most promising start to my Davis Cup adventure, though, losing my first two games, a singles and a doubles, against the Czechs. It was the toughest possible surface for me, meaning the fastest: hard court and indoors, where the air resistance is lowest. But in the end I emerged as the hero, winning the final and decisive match. Overall, I hadn't covered myself in glory and might very well have been singled out ("What was he doing there at that age?") as the reason for our defeat, but when you win the game that clinches victory by the narrowest Davis Cup margin, 3–2, everything else is forgotten, luckily for me.

We then played Holland and won, but no thanks to anything I did, since the one game I played in, a doubles, we lost. But the semifinal against what was then a strong France team was something else altogether. It was my first time representing Spain in Spain, in the Mediterranean city of Alicante, with a local crowd roaring its support in a way I had never felt before. We had a strong team, led by Carlos Moyá and Juan Carlos Ferrero, who were in the top ten, and Tommy Robredo, who was number twelve in the world rankings. I won my doubles match but, in such company, was not expecting to be picked by our captains to play in the singles. I wasn't, but Carlos suddenly felt unwell, and on his advice, they named me in his place. I won my match and I won it well, and we went through to the final against the United States.

Until then, I hadn't felt as nervous as I should have been. If I had been older, I would have been more aware of the national weight of expectation on my shoulders. I look back on it now and I see myself playing almost recklessly, more adrenaline than brains. But I sobered up and gulped when I saw the stadium where we were going to be playing the final. It was in the beautiful city of Sevilla, but not in the most beautiful of settings. The Centre Court at Wimbledon it wasn't, nor was I going to be hearing the echo of my shots once the hostilities began. Silence was not going to be on the agenda. Nor were we going to feel remotely cushioned or enclosed. They'd improvised a court in one half of an athletics stadium around which they were going to seat 27,000 people: the biggest audience ever to watch a game of tennis. Add to that the Sevillanos' famed exuberance and you could well and truly forget the hushed reverence of Wimbledon, or for that matter anywhere else I'd ever played before. This was going to be tennis played before a crowd of screaming football fans. Although, going into the final, I was only down to play one doubles match, and although I was going to share the load with Tommy Robredo (who, as senior partner here, would actually be carrying a disproportionate share of the responsibility for success or failure), at my eighteen and a half years I felt more pressure and more tension than I had ever felt in my long decade of relentless competition. Our rivals were the twin brothers Bob and Mike Bryan, the world number ones and quite possibly the best doubles pairing ever. We were not expected to win, but the sense of occasion just in the buildup, the mood in the city, the excitement every time people saw us, was unlike anything I had ever imagined witnessing on the eve of a game of tennis.

I had far from given up hope, but the calculation our captains made was that we'd lose the doubles match, giving one point out of a possible total of five for the Americans, and that much would rest on Carlos Moyá, our number one, winning both his singles games. He'd beat Mardy Fish, the number two American; but beating Roddick was by no means a foregone conclusion. The advantage we had was that we were playing on clay, our favorite surface—not Roddick's. But he was a formidable competitor, a high-voltage American, and he was world number two, ahead of Carlos, who was then number five. The betting was on Carlos, who would be playing before his own fans, but it was by no means a safe bet. Juan Carlos Ferrero, who was 25 in the rankings (but he was better than that, injuries that year had brought him down) was expected to beat Fish, but against Roddick the odds seemed fifty-fifty. The critical thing was to win both our matches against Roddick, because we really did think we had the beating of Fish, twice.

Those were the numbers, anyway. That was the logic. But what if Fish did win one of his matches? It would not have been the biggest surprise in the game's history. We'd all suffered surprise defeats in our time (Carlos had lost to me that year, so he could certainly lose to Roddick), and complacency was far, far from our thoughts. Where we all agreed was that the first game on the first day against Roddick, our number two against their number one, would be massively important. If Carlos beat Fish and we won that one, we need not worry about Tommy and me failing to pull off our own surprise in the doubles, and we'd only have to win one of our two singles matches on the third and final day. With the pressure eased, Carlos's chances of beating Roddick in the matchup of the number ones would surely improve. And even if Carlos were to lose, the pressure on Fish, knowing that if he lost, the U.S. was beaten, would be another major factor in our favor.

So the big game, as we saw it on the day before the matches began, was the one between our number two and Roddick. And our number two was supposed to be Juan Carlos Ferrero, French Open winner and US Open finalist in 2003. Except that he wouldn't be our number two. It would be me; me against Roddick on day one. And not because he had an injury, but because our three captains decided I should play in his place. Instead of watching on the sidelines, giving my teammates all the energy and encouragement I could muster, I had suddenly been selected to take center stage. Our captains' boldness, or rashness (as many people saw it), came as an enormous surprise and shock to me. Juan Carlos had reached number one in the world rankings while I had never advanced beyond 50. Besides, Tommy Robredo, my doubles partner, was ranked 13. The entirely natural thing would have been for Tommy to play if Juan Carlos didn't. I was the kid in the team, there almost as much as a cheerleader as anything else, the way most people inside and outside the team saw it, for this grown-up business of a Davis Cup final against the United States of America.

Now, for all the camaraderie, tennis is an individual game, and we all want a chance to play. No one would have believed me if I'd said I preferred not to. The pressure and the responsibility excited me more than it scared me. If I'd felt any urge to run away, I might as well have quit professional tennis there and then. No, this was the biggest opportunity of my life to date and I was so thrilled at the prospect of playing I could hardly breathe. But I felt uncomfortable and apologetic. I was young and brazen enough to feel I could beat

Roddick, but I was not so crass as to fail to see that pitting me against him would be a violation of the natural order of things. My family had instilled in me a reverence for people older than myself, and these two teammates I'd been selected over were not only my elders, they were also—by any objective light—my betters. It was true that I had been playing well in training that week and Ferrero had been a little below par, but we all knew well enough too that training was one thing, the heat of competition something else. In a game as big as this, experience counted as much as current form, and if Ferrero wasn't the one, then Robredo, who was four years older than me and a winner of two ATP titles (to my zero at this point), was surely who should replace him.

The reality was that I was by some distance the lowest in the world rankings of our four team members; I'd had a bad year, for much of which I had been out with an injury; I had recently been beaten badly by Roddick; and I was eighteen years old. Besides, I'd have more chances to play in future Davis Cups than all of them, so if I put myself in Juan Carlos's and Tommy's shoes, I could see how playing in this final might mean even more to them than to me. Things became quite tense inside our group, and so I decided that rather than put the captains on the spot I'd go and talk to Carlos about it. I'd already known him for some years. We had practiced together many times. I trusted him as if he were an elder brother. And he was one of my own, a Mallorquín.

I asked him, "Wouldn't you feel more comfortable, more confident, honestly, if Juan Carlos were to play? I mean, I'm so young and he's won so much more than me . . ." Carlos cut me short. I remember his words exactly, "Don't be a dumb ass. You go ahead and play. You're playing well. For me, there's no problem at all." We talked a little more, I continued to remonstrate a bit, arguing the case against myself, conveying how embarrassed I felt. But he said, "No. Take it easy. Enjoy the moment, take the opportunity. If the captains have decided to put you in it's because they've thought about it long and hard and they trust you. I do too."

That settled it. It would have been ridiculous to carry on insisting I should not have played. First, because, in truth, I was dying to; second, because it would have meant questioning our captain's judgment, which it was definitely not my place as a teenager to do. The extreme option, a principled rebellion, would have been too stupid for words.

So I played, going on court after Carlos had done me the additional favor of winning the first match. If I beat Roddick, we wouldn't win the Davis Cup, but we'd have a big foot in the door; if I lost, it would all be up for grabs. I was as motivated as I had ever been, fully aware that this was, without a shadow of a doubt, the biggest match of my young life. I was also afraid—afraid that I would not be up to the challenge, that Roddick would give me the same beating he'd given me in the US Open, that he'd win 6–3, 6–2, 6–2, something like that. That would be embarrassing and no help to the team whatsoever. Because you can lose but at least tire him out along the way, drain him for the next match. But if he thrashed me again, I'd have failed the captains who had placed such faith in me, my teammates, the public, everybody. It was a very high-pressure match for me. It was the Davis Cup final, on Spanish soil; I wasn't playing for myself alone; and, yes, above all, what caused me the greatest fear was that very risky decision they'd made to pick me.

But when I went out on court, the adrenaline pushed the fear away, and the crowd swept me along on a tide of such emotion that I played in a rush of pure instinct, almost without pausing to think. Never has a crowd been more behind me, before or since. Not only

was I the Spaniard flying the flag in one of the most fervently patriotic cities in Spain, I was the underdog, the David to Roddick's Go-
liath. Anything further removed from Wimbledon's fine sense of
tennis etiquette (silence during points: forget it) it would be hard to
imagine. I'd never achieve my childhood dream of becoming a professional footballer, but this was the closest I'd ever get to feeling
the atmosphere a football player feels walking out onto the stadium
for a big match, or scoring a goal in a championship decider. Except
that here every time I won a point, practically, all 27,000 people
erupted as if I'd scored a goal. And I have to admit that I quite often
responded as if I were a footballer who'd just scored. I don't think
I've ever pumped my arms in the air or jumped in celebration more
often during a game of tennis. I am not sure how Andy Roddick felt
about it, but there was no other way to respond to the festive
energy that washed down on me. A tennis crowd rarely has much
influence on the result compared to a football or basketball crowd.
Here they did. I'd always known about the benefits of home advantage, but I'd never felt it before; I'd never quite known the lift a
crowd can give you, how the roar of support can transport you to
heights you had no idea you could reach.

I needed the help. Blood wasn't spilled, but it was a battle we
waged out there, Roddick and I, in that amazing amphitheater, in
the warm winter sunshine of Sevilla. It would be the longest match
I'd played in my life up to that moment, three hours and forty-five
minutes of long, long rallies, constant slugging back and forth, with
him looking for opportunities to charge to the net and me almost
always holding back on the baseline. Even if I'd lost, I'd have done
my bit for the cause, exhausting him for the match two days later
against Carlos, who'd won his first game comfortably. And I did lose
the first set, which went to a tiebreak, but this only encouraged the

crowd even more, and I ended up winning the next three sets, 6–2, 7–6, and 6–2. I remember a lot of points well. I remember in particular a return I made to a very wide-angled second serve that went round, not over the net, for a winner. I remember a backhand passing shot in the tiebreak of the third set, a critical moment in the match. And I remember the final point, which I won on my serve when he hit a backhand long. I fell on my back, closed my eyes, looked up, and saw my teammates dancing for joy. The noise in my ears felt like a jumbo jet flying low overhead.

We were 2–0 up in the five game series; we lost the doubles, as predicted, the next day; and on the third day Carlos Moyá, who was our real hero, and who had been chasing this prize for years, won his match against Roddick—and that was that. I didn't have to play Mardy Fish. We'd won 3–1 and the Davis Cup was ours. It was the highlight of my life and also, as it turned out, the moment when the tennis world stood up and started paying close attention to me. Andy Roddick said something very nice about me afterward. He said that there weren't many truly big game players, but that I definitely was a big game player. It had certainly been big pressure I'd had to overcome, after the controversy of me being chosen to play Roddick, and it gave me new confidence on which to build for when the time came to play big games, Grand Slam finals, all alone.

You're the sum of all the games you've played, and while that Davis Cup final was far from my thoughts three and a half years later, as I tried to win the third set at Wimbledon's Centre Court against Federer, it had left its mark. At least it had helped in the first two sets, which I'd won. But he had begun this set playing some brilliant shots, and I was on the ropes, nowhere more so than in the sixth game, on my serve, when I went 15–40 down after playing a really disappointing backhand into the net. For the first time in the match I lost my cool, letting out a cry of rage. I was angry with myself because I knew perfectly well I had not done what I should have done on that shot. I cut it when I should have driven it. My head had failed me. I knew that was not the shot to hit, but I had a moment's hesitation, a moment of fear, and hit it anyway. I went for the conservative option, I lost my courage. And at that moment, I hated myself for that. The good news was that Federer was on edge too. It was a tremendously tense game for both of us but, for that very reason, it was not the most dazzling game of the match in terms of the quality of the tennis. We were both playing poorly at the same time. The difference was that I played less poorly when it mattered the most. He had four break points in the sixth game, each of which I defended successfully, until finally I got an advantage and won the game, on my second serve.

And so we were at 3–3 with him serving, the famous "crucial" seventh game coming up. It's not always as crucial as tennis lore has it, not at all, but this time it was: I saw my opportunity and I felt I was ready to take it. He had to have been rattled by his failure to capitalize on the chances he'd had in the previous game. At this point overall in the match he'd had twelve break points to my four, but he'd taken one and I'd taken three. Here was evidence of how tennis matches turn on the big points, of how the difference between victory and defeat lies not in physical strength or native ability but in having the psychological edge. And that was on my side of the court right now; the tension was at its highest, but the momentum had shifted. Suddenly, having survived the pressure he had been piling on me the game before, I was feeling fleet-footed and sharp. Looking up, I saw the sky was heavily overcast, not a shadow on court. It seemed as if it really was going to rain after all. All the more reason to try and kill off the match now.

And that was what everything suggested I was about to do. Three times he came to the net and three times I won the point. He was rushing things, losing his cool. I was 0–40 up. I heard a cry of support from where my uncles and aunt were sitting. *"Vamos Rafael!"* I glanced up to acknowledge I'd heard them. But then, in the blink of an eye, the tables turned again. It was I who succumbed to the pressure. I made a poor return of serve, short to mid-court, and handed him the point. Next, I failed to return a serve. But it was a good serve, so on to the next point. I had one last chance to break before he could get back to deuce. Here, at 30-40, was the point in this match that I never forget. A terrible memory. He missed his first serve, hit a perfectly returnable second to my forehand, and I fluffed it completely, into the net. It was my third chance, having lost the previous two, and fear gripped me. I lacked decision, my head was not clear. That was a test of mental endurance, and I failed it, that's why I remember it so painfully. I failed where I had trained myself all my life to be strongest. And once again, I caught myself thinking, "I may not get this chance again; this might be the turning point of the match." I knew I had lost a big chance right there to win Wimbledon, or to come very close to winning it.

And, sure enough, two great serves and he won the game. It was a huge disappointment, but I had to wipe it out of my mind immediately. And I did. I won the next game comfortably and he did the next one on his serve. He was 5–4 up and then, as forecast, the rain came down. I was ready for this and took it calmly, even though more than an hour passed before we were able to restart. I marched to the locker room, where Toni and Titín promptly joined me. Titín changed the bandages on my fingers and I changed my clothes. We said very little. I was in no mood for talking. Federer was looking more relaxed, chatting and even laughing a bit with his people. He was down two sets, but I was more tense than he was. Or looked more tense, at any rate.

Back on court, I served to save the set and did so; and two games later saved the set again. We went to a tiebreak and he killed me with his serving, ending the set as he'd begun it. Three aces, plus another serve that might as well have been one, gave him the tiebreak by seven points to five and the set, 7–6. I'd had my chance, and through a couple of moments of weakness when I should have been strongest, I'd thrown it away. But I was still two sets to one up.

HIGHLY STRUNG

YOU DIDN'T NEED especially fine antennae on the eve of the Davis Cup Final of 2004 to spot the disgruntlement in the faces of Juan Carlos Ferrero and Tommy Robredo, denied their places in history by the eighteen-year-old upstart Nadal. It was obvious to anybody watching the team press conference the night before the first day of play, seeing the foursome pose for photographs, that the Spanish team was not a portrait of patriotic harmony. Carlos Moyá, Spain's number one, spoke with ambassadorial poise; Ferrero and Robredo looked as if they would rather be somewhere else; Nadal fidgeted, stared at his feet and forced smiles that did little to disguise his unease.

"When Rafa came to me and said he was willing to cede his place in the match against Roddick to one of the two older guys, I said no, that was the captains' call and, anyway, he had my full confidence. But inside," Moyá recalls, "I had my doubts." Moyá transmitted the same message to Toni Nadal, who was also uncomfortable. "The decision had been made," Moyá said, "and I saw no point in causing even more tension in the group, and adding to the pressure on Rafa, who was in a dilemma, by saying anything else."

Moyá spoke bluntly to Ferrero, asking him to take the decision on the chin and remember that he had played his part in getting Spain to the final. The Davis Cup record books would show that, and wins for him and Nadal would mean victory for him too. Whether they bought the argument or not, Rafa's doubts as to the legitimacy of him playing was now an added factor of concern for Moyá. Had Rafa been more brash, less sensitive, had he either not picked up on, or simply not been bothered by, the ill feeling that suddenly plagued the group, he would at least have been going into the decisive match against the experienced American number one in a less cluttered frame of mind. But that was not the case. Moyá knew very well that beneath the gladiatorial front he put on during a match there lurked a wary, sensitive soul; he knew the Clark Kent Rafa the indecisive one who had to hear many opinions before he could make up his mind, the one afraid of the dark, frightened of dogs. When Nadal visited Moyá at home, Moyá had to lock his dog up in a bedroom, otherwise Nadal would be completely incapable of settling down.

He was a highly strung young man alert to other people's feelings, accustomed to a protected and harmonious family environment, out of sorts when there was bad blood. Spain's Davis Cup family was distinctly out of sorts now, and making things worse, Nadal was—if not the cause—certainly at the heart of the problem. Getting his head in order for the biggest match of his life, Moyá sensed, was going be a bigger challenge than usual for his young friend. As if that were not bad enough, Moyá could not help reminding himself that Rafa, however sharp he might have looked in training that week, had lost just fourteen days earlier against a player ranked 400 in the world. And his serve was conspicuously weaker than Roddick's, which was almost 50 percent faster.

But Moyá did also have reasons to believe in his young team-mate. He had known Rafa since he was twelve years old, had trained with him scores of times, and had been beaten by him two years earlier in an important tournament. No top professional had been closer to Rafa, and none would continue to remain on more intimate terms with him, than his fellow Mallorcan. Ten years older than Nadal, Moyá, who had briefly snatched the number one spot from Pete Sampras in 1999, knew that Nadal had special qualities; but just how special he would not find out until after the youngster had gone out in front of 27,000 people at Seville's converted athletics stadium, all the pressure in the world on his shoulders, and played the world number two in four physically grinding, emotionally supercharged sets.

"People were already talking about Rafa in Mallorca when he was six or seven years old," says Moyá, "although at first you had to wonder if it was because his uncle was Miguel Ángel, the football player, who was a legend on the island. But the tennis world is small there—my trainer, Jofre Porta, used to do some coaching with him too—and after he'd won the Mallorca under-12s championship at the age of eight, a buzz began to be generated around him. I remember Jofre telling me, 'This one's going to be good.' By the age of twelve he was already one of the best in the world in his category. That was when I met him for the first time."

The meeting took place in Stuttgart, Germany. Moyá was play-ing in an ATP tournament, Nadal in a junior one. "Someone from Nike, who'd already had the smarts to sign him up, asked me if I'd warm up with him. I did, for about an hour. Now, to be honest, he did not strike me as being singularly more gifted than other players of his age. I did see he was very combative, though what was more surprising was how incredibly shy he also was. We met and shook hands, but he didn't even look at me and uttered barely a syllable. It's true he was probably a bit overawed, since I'd made a bit of a splash in the media after making it, unseeded, to the Australian Open final earlier that year. But the contrast was still striking—shocking, actually—between the timid little boy off court and the super-competitive kid on it, even though we were just rallying, not even playing points."

When he was fourteen, by which time Moyá had won his one and only Grand Slam tournament, the French Open, he began training with Moyá in Mallorca, as often as three times a week. "People sometimes say to me, 'You've helped Rafa a lot, right?' Well, maybe, but he's helped me a lot too. Those training sessions were of value to me too. He was good enough already to push me hard, even though I was well established by now in the world top ten. We played sets together, and since I didn't want to lose against a kid of fourteen, he helped me keep my edge. I even think he helped make me a better player."

The reverse was more obviously true. Few aspiring professionals, if any, in the history of the game can have had the good fortune to practice on a regular basis at the age of fourteen with a player who had won a Grand Slam tournament and who, when he was away on tour, was frequently competing with such tennis deities as Pete Sampras and Andre Agassi. It was another example of how kindly the stars had been aligned for the young man who dreamed of being a champion.

There was the original good luck of having had an uncle who, after failing to achieve his own tennis-playing dreams, dedicated himself life and soul to building a player capable of competing mentally and physically at the highest level. There was the warm, doting, remarkably close remainder of the family to act as a counterweight to the uncle's fiercely disciplined regime. There was his uncle Miguel Ángel, whose sporting celebrity provided an example, right on his doorstep, of the importance of training hard and of how to stay centered, however much acclaim came his way. And then there was Carlos Moyá. Stumbling across a mentor, confidant, and practice partner of such stature and generosity would be beyond the dreams of an aspirant professional raised in New York, London, or Madrid, but in the hermetic tennis environment of a small island like Mallorca, whose natives by nature stick together, it could happen, and it did.

Moyá, who has a home in Miami and another in Madrid and is much more cosmopolitan by nature than Nadal, made the kid from Manacor his pet project. Nadal's parents gush when they talk about Moyá, noting that a lesser character than he might have run off in the opposite direction at the sight of the young pretender, all the faster the more threatening to his dominion he became. Yet the more successful Nadal became—as he progressively usurped Moyá's status as king of Mallorca, king of Spain, and king of the tennis world—the warmer the relationship between the two became. Nadal regards him to this day as the wise and benevolent big brother he never had. He has continued to confide in Moyá and seek advice from him to a degree that he can with no one else outside his family circle, with the possible exception of his physiotherapist and resident de facto psychologist, the man he calls Titín.

"I did like to feel in the beginning that I was helping a boy to achieve his dream and I felt motivated by the idea of being a mirror in which he might see himself," says Moyá, who admits that before long it was Nadal who would be motivating him. "I could see, by the sheer intensity with which he trained, that he was super-ambitious and desperate to improve. He hit every shot as if his life depended on it. I've never seen anything like it, not even close. You compared him with other kids his age and, well, it was exactly what you see now that he has become one of the greats of the tennis circuit. Sure, at that age you never know what's going to happen. The world is full of sportsmen and -women who looked like world beaters at the age of fourteen and, for whatever circumstances of life or hidden weaknesses of character, sank without a trace. What was certain about Rafa was that he had something different."

And he had an audacity that belied his self-effacing demeanor off court. "He began playing the Futures tournaments, the junior competitions of the ATP, at fifteen," said Moyá, "playing at times against players ten years older than he was. I worried at first that for a boy accustomed to winning, the inevitability of losing—and losing often—would sap his confidence. That was the danger. One more time, I underestimated him. Within five months he started winning games; within eight or nine, tournaments."

Moyá is amazed at the speed with which Nadal "burned through" the normal stages of tennis evolution. "When I was fifteen, I played summer tournaments in Mallorca and went to school in winter. That was my limit. If I'd started playing Futures matches then, I'd have lost 6–0, 6–0 every time. As it was, I started at seventeen and that was what happened.

"After a year, when he was sixteen, he moved up from the Futures to the Challengers competition, one step below the full-on ATP circuit. At first it was tough for him. He was playing on indoor hard courts, the fastest surface there is—a million miles removed, in tennis terms, from the clay courts in the humid, hot environment where he was raised. Typically we Spanish perform badly on those courts, and at first he suffered too. In fact, Spanish players often don't even bother to turn up, because they know from experience that the chances are they'll be out in the first round.

"The first time we'd played a competitive match against one another he was sixteen and I was twenty-six. It was in Hamburg, a big ATP Masters tournament, early in 2003. In the many practice games we'd had over the previous couple of years I almost always won. I'd say, in fact, that if I really wanted to win, I always did. Not surprisingly. But on this occasion I was nervous. I felt incredibly pressured. I was in the top ten, he was a kid, an emerging star, sure, but ranked 300 or so. Losing would be an embarrassment, and I felt that pressure keenly.

"It was a night game, it was cold. I felt the cold but he seemed not to; he seemed to be hot before we'd even played the first point. Actually, he didn't play at his best. And nor did I. But he beat me, in two sets. It was as clear-cut a case as you'll find of a player winning through superior mental strength. You'd see other kids of sixteen on the circuit who were not as good as he was but with a far more cha- otic attitude on court, raging away at the slightest setback. What I saw across the net from me that day was a player who was very tal- ented indeed but, above all, one whose concentration, professional- ism, focus were on another level from mine. Someone whose weak game was ten times stronger than any equivalent player's weak game. And—I say this just to show how remarkable this was—don't forget that by now I'd won a Grand Slam and had been a finalist at the Australian Open.

"At the end of the match we hugged at the net and he said, 'I'm sorry.' He needn't have said it. I took the loss more philosophi- cally than I might have expected beforehand. I knew that this was going to be the first of many defeats; that Rafa was the future and I, while far from finished, was beginning my descent."

As the years went by, and one rose and the other fell, Moyá became increasingly aware of the intimidating effect Nadal had on other players. "I don't think he would ever admit it, and I've never asked him about it, but I do believe that he does deliberately intimidate rivals," Moyá says. "He is more complex and vulnerable in private than he lets on in public, but the effect he has on his rivals is not complex at all. They are daunted by him. Those rituals he has: they're a show in themselves. You don't see any other player do anything like it. And as for his physical preparation, he goes out on court practically sweating, something I never managed to do, but it is the ideal condition in which to start a match."

Carlos Costa, Rafa's agent and also a former pro, agrees with Moyá that there is something scary about coming up against Nadal, describing his impact on his rivals, like the impact Tiger Woods at his best had on the rest of the professional golf world, as that of the dominant alpha male over the rest of the pack. "Towards the end of my career I played against him competitively," Costa says, "and, yes, there came a point in a match when fear entered your heart. You knew you were in the presence of a born winner. Rafael is stronger mentally than everybody else; he's made of special stuff."

He also has a special charisma. Moyá, a big star in his day, had been Spain's first ever world number one, but long before Nadal himself even made it to number two, the younger man had outstripped him in popular appeal, in his own country and beyond. Moyá was more classically good-looking (in May 1999 *People* magazine put him in its list of "the 50 most beautiful people in the world"), but he could not match Nadal's elemental appeal; Moyá was a more elegant player, with a more powerful serve, but Nadal's ferocious competitiveness had more seductive force. He connected with the public in a way that Moyá never could.

Moyá calmly accepts this because he knows he is not, nor ever was, in the same league as Nadal. Not in terms of talent, but in terms of attitude. "It's Rafa's head that distinguishes him from the rest. That comes through on court, not just for his rival but also for people watching on TV. It's invisible but you feel it. His backhand, his forehand: others have that. Of course he is talented. I think he doesn't realize himself how much, because he has a tendency to underestimate himself. But in terms of mentality, he is out of this world. I've known many top athletes, not just in tennis, and nobody has what he has—with the exception maybe of Tiger Woods or Michael Jordan. He is an assassin on the crucial points; his concentration is absolute, and he has something I never had, an ambition without limits. I won one Grand Slam, I was happy: my life's work was done. Rafa needs to win more and more and he'll never have enough.

"He has the same hunger in each point. I was 5–0 up in a set: my mind would wander; I gave away a game, two. Rafa, never. He gives nothing away for free; he conveys to his rivals the crushing, disheartening message that he is going to do all he can to beat you 6-love, 6-love."

Yet that is not, for Moyá, the whole story, which he says is more layered and complex. Nadal does have a flaw. And one connected in Moyá's mind with that ambiguity between his sensitive, insecure private self and the sporting battering ram the world sees. In Moyá's view, Nadal does not entirely shed his Clark Kent persona on court; the transformation to Superman, willed as it is and convincing as it looks, is not complete. "He is more cautious than you might think on court. He has always been wary of his second serve, and that is why he does not hit his first as hard he could, given how powerful his physique is. You see the same caution in his open play. I've trained with him a thousand times on court, and I'm always struck when I see him play a match by how much more aggressive he is in training, how many more winners he hits. I've said to him many times, 'Why don't you loosen up more? Why not play more inside the court and go on the attack more, at least in the early rounds of tournaments, when you often come up against players you could beat with your eyes shut?' But he doesn't, or does so less often than he should. Maybe in part because of that refusal of his to believe how good he really is."

Moyá believes that Nadal's warrior image comes not so much from his attacking aggression as from his never-say-die defensiveness. He plays with the spirit of the Alamo, a sensation that transmits itself to the crowds, to whom he conveys the impression, no matter his standing in the world rankings, that he is playing the part of the defiant underdog. As Moyá says, Federer would never be seen as a gladiatorial figure because he is not a battler, a scrambler; he is not fighting for his life as Nadal always seems to be doing. Federer's trademark is his lethal precision.

That Nadal has proved such a resilient champion has all the more merit, in Moyá's eyes, for the anxieties he has had to overcome to get there. It also helps account for his magnetic on-court persona. People connect more with the battling underdog than with the effortlessly superior performer, because the battling underdog is more recognizably human; more people see themselves in the flawed Nadal than in the Olympian Federer. They would do so less if he were more like the past master with whom he is sometimes compared, Björn Borg; or if he were as wildly exuberant on court as John McEnroe was. For Moyá, Nadal is a cross between the two players who staged the greatest rivalry tennis had seen until Nadal and Federer came along. Borg was pure ice, McEnroe was all fire. "The secret of the tremendous appeal he has worldwide," says Moyá, "is that you can see he is as passionate as McEnroe was, but he has the self-control of Borg, the cold-blooded killer. To be both in one is a contradiction, and that's what Rafa is."

Me as a baby, offering
a glimpse of an obsession
to come.

Me as a toddler, cooling off under
the Mallorcan sun.

In the uniform of Real Madrid,
the football team of my life.

I get an early taste of another
of my life's pleasures: boating.

Me with my uncle Miguel Ángel Nadal,
the professional soccer player.

In costume . . .

Me with pals, all coached by my uncle Toni.

Reflecting on the game.

With Boris Becker
and friends.

Doing speed and agility
training in Manacor, age
sixteen. *(© Joan Forcades)*

Me and tennis-playing Goofy.

Tests and training in
the gym in Mallorca.
(© Joan Forcades)

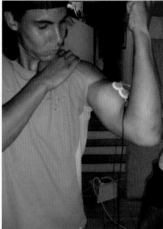

Me with the French Open trophy in Paris, 2008, with, from left to right, at back: my father, my mother, Rafael "Titín" Maymó. Front: Benito Pérez Barbadillo, Jordi "Tuts" Robert.
(© Jordi Robert)

Titín, Tuts, me, Carlos Costa, and Toni at the gardens of Versailles Palace (left to right) before the French Open, 2008.
(© Jordi Robert)

Tuts, Titín, me (left to right)
at a Japanese restaurant
in Melbourne during
the Australian Open, 2009.
(© *Jordi Robert*)

Titín, Tuts, Carlos Costa, me, my father, Toni
(left to right) in Melbourne, Australia, 2009.
(© *Jordi Robert*)

My father,
Benito Pérez,
Tuts, Carlos
Costa, me,
my sister,
my mother
(left to right).
With the trophy
certifying my
number one
world ranking
in 2010.
(© *Jordi Robert*)

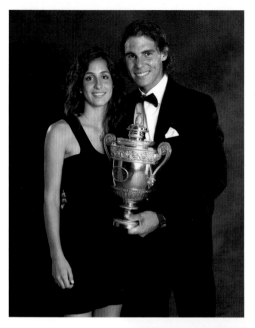

Me with my girlfriend, María Francisca Perelló, at the official dinner celebrating my Wimbledon victory in 2010.
(*Bob Martin/AELTC*)

At the house my team rents in Wimbledon, June 2010. Benito Pérez, Titín, Tuts, me.
(© *Jordi Robert*)

In Acapulco in 2005, en route to winning my first Grand Slam, the French Open. Me, Joan Forcades, Carlos Moyá (then in world top ten).
(© *Joan Forcades*)

CHAPTER 5

FEAR OF WINNING

INNING WIMBLEDON WAS an enticing enough prospect in itself, but I also knew that victory here would mean I'd soon be taking over as world number one for the first time, after two years following in Federer's footsteps. Defeat would mean me remaining at his shoulder, maybe condemned never to overtake him. But in this match I was in the lead, and I served at the start of the fourth set feeling as composed as one might reasonably hope to in such circumstances. Which is not very much, but at least my legs were not trembling and the adrenaline was still winning the battle against the nerves. Losing the third set on a tiebreak had been a blow, but that was history now. I knew he couldn't keep on delivering aces on every service game as he had done in the third set. I'd rated my chances before the match at fifty-fifty, and that hadn't changed.

There had been a time, after all, when I had rated my chances at scarcely above zero against him, and won. It was our very first encounter, on a fast court in Miami in March 2004. I was seventeen and he, aged twenty-two, had just made it to number one in the world rankings, but I beat him in straight sets. A year later we met in the final of the same tournament, and this time he won, but it was mighty close. I won the first two sets; he won the third on a tiebreak, and then he took the final two sets. It was a defeat, but an encouraging defeat. I was thirty places below Federer in the rankings but had gone toe to toe with him right to the end. After that, my career took off like a rocket: by the time the French Open came around, two and a half months later, I had climbed to world number five.

Immediately after Miami, I played in the tournament that marks the start of the clay court season, Monte Carlo. I love Monte Carlo, both the place and the tournament. It's on the Mediterranean and near home. The courts you play on hang high over the sea, so high I almost imagine I can see Mallorca from there. And the streets are so clean. What stays with me about the city is how impeccably ordered and tidy everything is. The tournament itself is one of my favorites, not just because I do well there and historically it has a special meaning for me, but because it has tradition, like Wimbledon. They've been playing it for more than a hundred years and many of the great names in the game have won there, such as Björn Borg, Ivan Lendl, Mats Wilander, and Ilie Nastase, as well as early greats of the Spanish game like Manuel Santana and Andrés Gimeno. My friend Carlos Moyá too.

I hadn't played in Monte Carlo the year before because of my foot injury, but I felt here was my chance, on the surface I'd grown up with, to win my first big ATP tournament. I'd let Miami slip, but I felt I wasn't going to let this one go. Not even if I came up against Federer again. I didn't, because he went out in the quarter finals and it was the defending champion, Guillermo Coria, from Argentina, who I played in the final.

Clay courts suit people with a defensive game. They also suit people who are fit. Tennis is a game that requires the speed of a

sprinter, sharp off the blocks, and the stamina of a marathon runner. You stop, start, stop, start. And you keep doing it over two, three,
four, sometimes as much as five hours. Games on clay last longer
because rallies last longer, because the ball bounces higher and stays
in the air longer, meaning it is harder to finish off points, and harder
to hold on to your serve. The endurance factor weighs more heavily
on the result than it does on other surfaces. The angles are wider, so
you have to cover more ground. It's more geometrical, as my physical
trainer, Joan Forcades, puts it. You have to build up a point gradually
and wait longer than on the faster surfaces to push your opponent
out of position, until the moment comes when you can realistically
think of attempting an unplayable winner. And it's a game too in
which you need to have a skill that is unusual in a game played
with a ball: skating, I call it. You're taught in tennis to balance your
weight solidly on the ground, positioning your feet and body in a
certain way, in order to strike a shot effectively, but in a high percentage of shots on clay the soft, gritty surface becomes momen-
tarily transformed into a skating rink, as you slide to reach the ball,
and all the usual rules go out of the window. If you haven't played on
clay from an early age, it is tough to master this skill. I had, having
learned the game on clay, and because I was fast and fit and never
gave up a ball for lost, this was a surface on which I knew that, once
I had reached a certain point of physical and mental maturity, I was
going to be hard to beat.

I won my first ever ATP tournament in Monte Carlo, beating
Coria in the final—an odd match in which I won in four sets but
lost the third 6–0—and then I went on a long unbeaten streak on
clay, winning in Barcelona and Rome. Next up after Rome was the
French Open in Paris, at Roland Garros, the climax of the clay court
season, the first Grand Slam of the year. I was number five in the

rankings but, still a little short of my nineteenth birthday, the favorite to win.

I hadn't played here the year before because of my injury, but I had flown up to watch the tournament for a couple of days. It had been the idea of Carlos Costa and my friend Tuts, my handler at Nike, who had organized the trip. Carlos thought it would be good for me to become familiar with the setting, at ease with it, because he thought this was a tournament I'd win one day. But I wasn't so much overawed as frustrated by my visit to the grand theater of French tennis. I hated not playing. I felt almost ill watching games involving people who I knew I had it in me to beat. Carlos still remembers me telling him, "Next year this one's mine." The greatest dream had always been Wimbledon, but I knew that a mountain I'd have to climb first would be Roland Garros. If I couldn't win in France, I'd never win in England.

But it still came as a surprise when the sports press made me the favorite to win the 2005 tournament. I'd only played in two Grand Slam tournaments, Wimbledon and the US Open, and I had not made it to the quarterfinals in either. There was a doubt in my mind, certainly, as to whether I'd be able to breathe at such a high competitive altitude. And, besides, Federer was there, and he only needed Roland Garros to complete his tally of four Grand Slams. Exaggerated and irrational as I tried to convince myself my status as favorite was (this was the part of my brain talking that Toni had conditioned), another part of me (the madly driven and ambitious one) did retain the conviction of a year earlier that I could win this. But the expectations I had generated did weigh on me, creating an added mental burden that I struggled to shed in the early rounds. I didn't have those good sensations I need to feel confident of winning and I felt far more nervous than usual. My body was tighter than it should have been.

My legs felt heavy, my arms stiffer, and the ball didn't come off the racket as crisply as it should have. When that happens, you become afraid to let fly, you don't give rein to your natural game, and everything becomes much more complicated. Rivals you've beaten comfortably in previous weeks suddenly become giants.

My diet wouldn't have helped either. I wasn't as careful as I am today to temper my appetites, and I'd suddenly acquired in Paris a fierce taste for chocolate croissants. Toni saw the problem, but he had his own special way of dealing with it. When Carlos Costa said to him, "For God's sake, don't let him eat that!" Toni replied, "No, no. Let him eat his chocolate cakes. That way he'll learn; that way he'll get a stomachache." As usual, his methods worked. I learned the hard way to avoid eating anything during a competition that could not be easily digested.

Despite the nerves and the self-imposed chocolate handicap, I managed to make it through those early rounds at the French Open. Francis Roig, my second coach, says that when I'm playing at 80 percent of my abilities, I'm better than the rest because of the mental edge I have over them. I'm not sure that is always true, but perhaps on clay it is. At my best I do have an ability to transform defense swiftly into attack, surprising, and even demoralizing, my opponent. But if the winners are not coming, if the best you can do is retrieve every shot, converting yourself into a human wall, then clay is where you want to be.

It was by grinding opponents down in this manner that I managed to make it to the semifinal against Federer, our first match on clay. It was the day of my nineteenth birthday and the best possible celebration, the best of my life, would be to win—which I did, in four sets. It was drizzling part of the time, and Federer, anxious to wrap up his Grand Slam foursome, tried to get the umpire to stop the game. It was a good sign. He said it was the rain that was getting to him, but I knew my game was too. The umpire didn't stop play and I won the match. Then it was Mariano Puerta of Argentina in the final. The Argentines are like the Spanish, experts on clay. And Puerta played better than me for long stretches of the match. I had not yet mastered the trick of isolating myself from my environment and from my fears. You never do fully, otherwise you wouldn't be human. But back then building the emotional defenses necessary to win consistently remained a work in progress, and the nerves tampered with my thought processes more than they would later in my career. What I didn't lack in that final was energy. Puerta was playing well, well enough to win the first set 7–5. But I think of that game now and what comes to mind is a sense of never having paused for breath. I was fighting and running as if I could fight and run for two days without rest. I was so excited at the thought of winning that I never felt a moment's tiredness, which in turn tired Puerta out. I held on; I was steadier on the big points, and I won every set after the first one, 6–3, 6–1, 7–5.

In the space of barely six months I'd climbed three peaks, one higher than the next. The Davis Cup, my first ATP win at Monte Carlo, and now, the headiest of all, the French Open, my first Grand Slam. The emotions I felt were indescribable. At the moment of victory I turned and saw my family going nuts, my parents hugging, my uncles screaming, and I understood immediately that, for all the years of hard work I had put in, this victory had not been mine alone. Without thinking, the first thing I did after shaking hands with Puerta was rush into the crowd and clamber up the steps to hug my family, Toni first among them. My godmother Marilén was there and she was crying. "I couldn't believe it," she told me later, recalling her reaction to the final point. "I looked at you there, a big, grown-up champion with his arms in the air, and suddenly my mind leapt back in time and I saw an image of a deadly serious, skinny little boy of seven training on a court back home in Manacor."

I had similar thoughts. I had battled so hard and long to get here. But into my mind there also came images of home with my family, and more than ever before, I understood that day that, however great your dedication, you never win anything on your own. The French Open was my reward, and my family's reward too.

I also felt relief. In winning a Grand Slam I'd taken a weight off my shoulders. Anything else that life brought now would be a welcome bonus. Not that I was going to ease up on my ambition. I had tasted victory at the highest level; I had liked it and wanted more. And I had a sense that after winning a tournament of this magnitude once, it would be less difficult to do it again. It was now, after winning at Roland Garros, that the idea began to take shape in my mind that I would win Wimbledon one day.

Needless to say, that was not Toni's thinking, or at least not the message he sought to transmit to me. With his usual bluntness, he told me he thought Puerta had played better than me, that he had made me run a lot more than I had him, and that I had been lucky to win the decisive points. He claims now—though honestly I don't remember this—that before heading back home before the rest of us the next day, he left a handwritten note for me with a list of all the aspects of my game I had to correct if I were to have any chance of winning a tournament this big again.

He was right as far as the year's two remaining Grand Slam tournaments were concerned. At Wimbledon I fell in the second round; at the US Open I fell in the third. Those defeats brought me down to earth and gave me a measure of the work still ahead if I was to avoid remaining just one more name in history's list of one-Slam

wonders, or yet another Spanish player incapable of adapting successfully to any surface that wasn't clay. The judgment of most experts after I won the French Open was that, while I might win this
tournament again, I'd never win one of the other three Grand Slam
tournaments, Wimbledon, the US Open, and Australia. They had
history to back them. We'd had one Spanish champion after another
at Roland Garros over the previous two decades but no victories in
the other big ones. In 2005 I had continued the trend, reinforcing the
prejudice.

But I was only nineteen, and whatever the future might hold, it
had been a spectacular year. I won a major tournament in Canada,
the Montreal Masters, beating André Agassi in straight sets in the
final, and then, at the end of the year, I won the Madrid Masters, a
tougher challenge on the fast surface that least suits my game: hard
court and indoors. Madrid was, in that respect, a watershed, a might-
ily encouraging sign that I did have it in me to adapt my game to
all conditions. In the final, I came back from two sets down to win
against a big-serving rival, Ivan Ljubicic of Croatia, whose game
was as naturally suited to playing indoors as mine was to clay.

All in all I won eleven tournaments in 2005, as many as Federer
that year, and I rose to number two in the world rankings. I was
starting to become well known beyond Spain and seemed poised to
take my game to another level. The year 2006 beckoned bright. Or
so I thought. Because after Madrid, calamity struck. I suffered an
injury to the same small bone in my foot that had obliged me to
miss the entire clay court season the year before. But this time it
was far more serious, turning out to be the most frightening episode by far in my professional career.

It was during the game against Ljubicic in Madrid on October
17 that I felt the first twinge. I didn't take it all that seriously at the

time, and accustomed as I was to competing in pain, I kept playing. That night it began to hurt a lot more, but I still wasn't alarmed. I thought it was the inevitable consequence of having played a hard five-set match and that the next day it would pass. But I woke up next morning and discovered the foot was more swollen than it had been the night before. I got out of bed, and placing the full weight of my body on the foot was impossible. Limping badly, I pulled out of the next tournament I was due to play, in Switzerland, and flew straight home to see my doctor, Ángel Cotorro. He didn't see anything especially serious, reckoning it was just a matter of time before the bone healed. Sure enough, a few days later I stopped limping and flew halfway across the world to Shanghai to take part in the year's big Masters tournament. But soon after I began training again the pain came back, so much so I had to withdraw from the tournament before it began. I flew back home and rested for two weeks, unable to do exercise of any kind. I resumed training, but on the second day I felt the flash of pain again and realized, with a despairing cry, that I simply couldn't go on.

I trust Dr. Cotorro with my life. He was my doctor then, he remains my doctor today, and if I have anything to do with it, he will remain my doctor till the day I retire. But he was unable to come up with a diagnosis, or with any advice beyond more rest. So that's what I did, for two more weeks. This was November, stretching now into December. I began to get nervous, because the doctor was trying everything yet couldn't figure out what exactly was wrong. The foot remained swollen and it was hurting more, not less. So then, at the suggestion of my uncle Miguel Ángel, we went to a foot specialist he had known during his time playing for Barcelona Football Club. The specialist carried out some resonance tests but had to admit that, for all his experience, the injury defeated him too. The last hope, as far as he could see, was that I should go and see an expert in Madrid who happened to have done a doctorate on the bone of the foot that was giving me the problem. I went along with my father, Toni, Joan Forcades, and Juan Antonio Martorell, my physical therapist prior to Titín. My left foot, or rather the little bone where the swelling was, had become the center of my anguished universe, and my family's too.

It was in a mood of rising alarm that in mid-December, two months after I had played my last competitive match, we fetched up at the consulting room of the Madrid doctor, who finally identified the problem. It should have been a relief, but it wasn't. The prognosis was so bleak that I sunk into the deepest, blackest hole of my life.

It was a congenital problem, a very rare disease of the foot, even more rare among men than women, in which the doctor happened to be a world specialist. He'd written a doctorate on the subject. The bone in question was called the tarsal scaphoid, located in the bridge of the foot, above the instep. If the tarsal scaphoid fails to ossify, or harden, as it should in early childhood, painful sequels are felt in adulthood, all the more so if the foot is submitted to repetitive stress of the kind that is inevitable if you are a professional tennis player. The danger is all the greater if, as was patently true in my case, you submit the foot to unusually intense activity during those early years when the bone is not yet fully formed. The consequence is that the bone becomes slightly deformed, bigger than it should be, and more liable to splinter, which was what had happened to me the year before. I had recovered from that but, being unaware of the problem, did not pay much attention to it, and now things had become a lot more complicated.

This defective tarsal scaphoid, a bone I'd never even known existed, turned out to be my own unique version of the Achilles' heel:

the most vulnerable point of my body, the most potentially destructive. Having diagnosed the problem, the specialist delivered his verdict. It could be, he pronounced, that I'd never be able to play competitive tennis again. I might be obliged to retire, at the age of nineteen, from the game in which I had invested my life's dreams. I broke down and wept; we all wept. But it was my father who gathered his wits first and sought to take control of the situation. While the rest of us stared helplessly at the floor, he sought out a plan. He is a practical man, my father, and he has the leader's instinct to appear calm and composed the more dire the circumstances become. By temperament cheerful, he has an attitude that sees no problem as insuperable. He's no athlete, but he has the mentality of a winner. That's why the rest of the family says that as a competitor I take after him. Maybe, but that day, as far away from a tennis court as I felt I had ever been, I felt neither cheerful nor practical. I was devastated. Everything I'd been building toward all my life was crumbling before my very eyes.

Amid the gloom, my father provided a tiny glimmer of light. He said two things: first, that he was confident we'd find a solution— the doctor's precise words, he reminded us, had been that the injury "might" be career threatening; second, and if all else failed, I could dedicate myself successfully to my new and growing passion, the game of golf. "With all that talent you have and all those guts," he said, "I see no reason why you couldn't turn yourself into a professional golfer."

That rather distant possibility would have to wait for now, and hopefully forever. The immediate question for the doctor was, might there be a solution, then? And if so, what? Short of surgery, a dicey and largely untested proposition, he said that there was one possibility. A rather banal, unmedical one. We could try adjusting the soles of my tennis shoes and, by a process of millimetric trial and error, see if we hit upon a shape that would provide the bone with the cushioning necessary to ease the pressure I had always put on the tarsal scaphoid. If that worked there was, he warned, a further risk: the subtle displacement of my body's weight caused by the refurbished soles might have a crippling impact on some other part of my body, such as my knees or my back.

My father lit up, said we'd cross that bridge when we came to it and immediately suggested a plan of action. We'd contact the foot specialist we had seen in Barcelona and get him to work right away with me and Dr. Cotorro on constructing the new soles. That said, my father, all brisk cheer, went off to a scheduled business dinner that very same night, leaving the rest of us in a mood that blended vague hope with funereal paralysis. After all the disappointments of the previous two months and the consistent failure of the bone to heal, there seemed to me to be little reason to believe the magical shoe solution would work. The foot hurt as much as it ever had, and, as I saw it, there was at most a faint chance the plan would work, but not enough to prevent me from going back home in a state of deepest gloom, preparing to spend what indeed turned out to be the bleakest Christmas ever.

I felt as if my life had been cut in half. When my family recall that period, they say I was completely transformed, unrecognizable. At home I'm normally in high spirits, laughing and joking a lot, especially with my sister. Now I became irritable, distant, dark. I didn't talk about the injury even to my closest friends; at first I couldn't bear even to open up about it with my girlfriend, María Francisca, who was growing baffled and alarmed by the change she saw in me. We'd just started going out a few months earlier, and here I was, a misery day and night, hardly an attractive proposition for a girl of seventeen eager to enjoy life. Typically so hyperactive, I couldn't even rest my foot on the ground, let alone think of playing tennis, and I'd lie for hours on end on the sofa staring into space, or sit in the bathroom, or on the stairs, weeping. I didn't laugh, I didn't smile, I didn't want to talk. I lost all appetite for life.

Thank God for my parents. Their response was just right. Making it plain that they were there for whatever I needed, they did not smother me. They didn't try to shake me out of my dark mood, they didn't bombard me with questions, they didn't try to get me to talk when I didn't want to. They ferried me here and there, to the doctor's or wherever, with the same uncomplaining cheerfulness my father had shown during the days when he had served as my untiring trans-Mallorcan chauffeur. They were sensitive and they were kind, and they made clear to me that they would stand by me in good times or bad, whether I ever got to play again or whether I'd have to find something else to do with my life.

Toni played his part too. It was he who shook me up, told me not to be so self-pitying. "Come on," he said, "let's go out and train." It sounded like madness, but he had a plan, even if it was not one exactly designed to win Wimbledon, or even the under-12s Balearic Islands championship. Following his instructions, I went out on court, hopping on crutches, sat down on a chair (a normal club chair—nothing specially designed), took a racket in my hand, and started hitting balls. So I wouldn't lose the habit, as Toni said. It was a psychological thing more than anything else. A way to pass the time, to stop dwelling on gloomy thoughts and try to build a little hope. Toni hit balls to me, from close up at first, then, as I got the hang of it, from the other side of the net; from my sitting position I'd hit back volleys, backhands, forehands. We varied the exercises as much as you could, in the circumstances, which was not much. But, as planned, it was good for my morale even if it didn't exactly improve my game, or do much good to my arms, either. We stuck at this curious regime, provoking a number of baffled looks from onlookers, for forty-five minutes a day over three weeks, and I'd always end up with my forearms stiff and sore. I did some swimming too, the one exercise I could do that involved my legs. But I'm not a good swimmer, and while it was good to be moving again, it was not a pastime that filled me with joy.

Resting the foot, resting it entirely, worked. The pain ebbed away. The tarsal scaphoid specialist in Madrid, whose diagnosis had initially been like a shot to the head, had turned out to be my salvation. After a lot of experimenting, we got the soles of the shoe right, or right enough to be getting along with. It wasn't the ideal solution for my body as a whole (we knew there would be consequences), but it did ease the problem of the scaphoid bone. The main thrust of the body's weight now fell on the other bones of my foot, relieving the pressure on the damaged one. Nike devised a shoe for me that was wider and higher than the one I used before. I needed a bigger shoe because the sole was now much thicker, more elevated, particularly in the area that now acted as a cushion for the scaphoid bone. Adapting to the new sole at first was uncomfortable, because by altering the region of the foot where the weight naturally falls, the shoe impaired my balance. And then, as the specialist had predicted, I started suffering muscle strains where I'd never had any problems before, in the back and thighs.

We did the best we could, but as I began training with the new shoes, new difficulties would keep cropping up, obliging us to keep on making tiny but critical changes to the soles. Years later, we still do. It's a work in progress. We still haven't got it absolutely right. Maybe there is no absolutely right solution. The fact is that years have passed since then, and the tarsal scaphoid bone still hurts me, obliging me at times to cut short training. It is the part of my body that Titín still spends the most time massaging. It remains under control, just, but we can never drop our guard.

The fabulous news was that by February I was back in full training. And that month, after nearly four months away, I played my first tournament, in Marseille. To go out on court, hear my name called out on the loudspeaker, see and hear the crowds, go out and start warming up again before a match: I'd been dreaming about this or, rather, almost not daring to dream about it, yet here I was back again. I hadn't won anything yet, but in the mere act of going out on court, I felt almost the same euphoria as if I had. I had recovered the life I thought I had lost, and never had I been so aware of the value of what I had, how immensely fortunate I was to be a professional tennis player, while understanding at the same time more clearly than ever before that the athlete's life is short, and can be cut shorter at any moment. There was no time to waste, and from now on I would seize with both hands every single opportunity that came my way. Because from that time on I saw that I would never know entirely for sure whether a match I was playing would be my last. This understanding led me to only one conclusion: I'd have to play each one, and train for each one, as if it *were* my last. I had come close to tennis death; I had stared the end of my career in the face, and the experience, awful as it had been, had made me stronger mentally, given me the wisdom to see that life—any life—is a race against time.

I was back in my stride far more quickly than I would have imagined possible, making it to the semifinals in Marseille and then winning my next tournament, in Dubai. There I beat Federer in the final, and on a hard court, the surface toughest on my foot.

It was a fantastic confidence boost, for I knew now I was back. A curious thing I discovered, and an encouraging one, was that the foot hurt a lot more in training than when I was competing in a tournament. Titín, whose judgment I trust in practically all things, had an explanation. He said this was because the adrenaline and the endorphins kick in during a match, acting as nature's pain-killer, but also because during a match I'm in a state of concentration so deep, I'm so removed from the rest of the physical world, that even if the discomfort is there I notice it less.

So one change we made after I came back from the injury was to train less. My physical trainer, Joan Forcades, had never been one to recommend long runs, something I know other tennis players do. When we did run, it would be for no more than half an hour or so. Now we cut out running altogether. Given that in normal circumstances I play about ninety matches a year, that in itself was quite enough to take care of my aerobic fitness. As a direct response to the fragility of my foot, we also cut back on the amount of training I did overall, both on court and physical training in the gym. Before the injury, until the age of eighteen, I'd do five hours a day or more; now I do three and a half, and less intensively than I used to. I don't practice for two hours at 100 percent; I play forty-five minutes at 100 percent, and I look for more specific things to work on, such as the volley or the serve.

I'll never stop being a player who fights for every ball. My style remains defense and counterattack. But if I look at videos of myself during, for example, the Davis Cup final of 2004, in the match against Andy Roddick, I see a scrambling dynamism you don't see quite so much in my game anymore. I am more measured; I economize more on my movements, and I have worked to improve my serve. It's still not my strongest point and remains distinctly weaker than Federer's and many other players'. But I did consciously work on it for my return to tennis in February 2006, and as Toni reminds me, there was a significant increase in speed. He says that before the injury I was serving at 160 kilometers per hour; in Marseille I served regularly at more than 200.

The faster serve should have helped me in the two big tournaments I always play in the U.S. early in the year, Indian Wells and Miami, but I failed once again in both. In Miami I fell in the very first round to my old friend Carlos Moyá. No favors there, but then again I had hardly been soft on him at our first meeting in Hamburg three years earlier.

And then it was back to the Mediterranean again. Returning to Monte Carlo that year was like coming home. I was back on clay, in the place where I'd won my very first ATP tournament. Once again I came up against Federer in the final, and once again I won. Then I faced him again in the final at Rome. It was a killer match, a true test of whether I had recovered from my injury. I had. The match went to five sets, lasted five hours; I saved two match points, and I won. And then it was Roland Garros and a chance I thought I'd never have just four months earlier of preserving my French Open crown. It meant more to me to be back here now than it had to be here the year before, even though that had been my first time. Winning this would mean, for me and my family, that the nightmare we'd gone through would be, if not forgotten, exorcised, and we could resume, in a clear and confident state of mind, the victorious trajectory that had been so nearly terminally curtailed. And I had a point to prove: I wanted to show that my win in 2005 had not been a one-off, that I was in the Grand Slam league to stay.

I made it to the final by a tough route, beating some of the top players of the moment, among them Robin Soderling of Sweden,

Lleyton Hewitt of Australia, and, in the quarterfinals, Novak Djokovic. A year younger than me, Djokovic was a hell of a player, temperamental but hugely talented. Toni and I had been talking about him and I'd been watching him in my rearview mirror, looming closer, for a while now. He'd been racing up the rankings, and I had a strong feeling that he would be neck and neck with me before too long, that it would not just be me, but me and him, against Federer. Djokovic had a strong serve and was fast and wiry and strong—often dazzling—on both forehand and backhand. Above all, I could see he had big ambitions and a winner's temperament. More a hard court than a clay court player, he was competitive enough to make it difficult for me in the Roland Garros quarters. I won the first two sets 6–4, 6–4, and was preparing for a long afternoon's work when unfortunately for him, but fortunately for me, he had to pull out with an injury.

In the final it was Federer again. I lost the first set 6–1, but won the next three, the final one on a tiebreak. Watching the video of the match later, I thought Federer played better than me overall, but in an atmosphere of high tension (he, so eager to complete the foursome of major titles; me, so desperate to banish the ghosts of my exile), I stuck it out.

As Carlos Moyá saw it, Federer was not fully Federer when he played against me. Carlos said I had beaten him by attrition, badgering him into untypical mistakes for a man of such enormous natural talent. That had been the plan, but I also think I won because I'd won the year before and that gave me a confidence I might otherwise have lacked, especially against Federer. Whatever the case, I'd won my second Grand Slam.

After all I had been through, it was an incredibly emotional moment. I ran up into the stands, as I had done the year before, and this time it was my father I sought. We hugged hard and we were both crying. "Thank you, Daddy, for everything!" I said. He doesn't like to show his feelings. He had felt the need to look strong and composed during my injury, but it was not until now that I fully grasped how hard he'd battled to stop himself from breaking down. Then I hugged my mother, who was also in tears. The thought that filled my mind at that moment of victory was that it was their support that had pulled me through. Winning the French Open in 2006 meant that we'd come through the worst; we'd overcome a challenge we feared might overwhelm us, and we had come out the stronger for it. For my father, I know, that was the moment of greatest joy of my entire career. As he saw it, if my foot had held out against the best of the best, it would continue to hold out for a good while to come. For him, who understood best of all what I'd gone through, it meant a return to life.

I could now realistically start thinking again about achieving my life's longstanding dream: winning Wimbledon. Carlos Costa remembers that my reaction to winning the French Open the first time, in 2005, had been, "Right, now for Wimbledon." At the time, he has since confessed, he thought I was setting my sights too high. He honestly didn't think I had it in me to win there. But after my victory at Roland Garros in 2006, when once again I declared that I was going to win Wimbledon, he told me he had begun to change his mind. Partly because grass was the most benign surface for my foot, but most of all because he had now convinced himself I had the temperament to win on such a stage. Carlos, who as a former top tennis player has a wary respect for the Grand Slams, did not think, on the other hand, that the other two big ones, the US Open and the Australian Open, were within my reach. But Wimbledon, yes. He joined me in the idea that I'd one day lift the golden trophy.

For all my outward confidence, the truth was that I lacked the necessary self-belief to win it when the chance came one month later. I did make it to the final at Wimbledon, but Federer beat me, more comfortably than the score line of 6-0, 7-6, 6-7, 6-3 suggested.

But now it was 2008, two years later, and I was two sets to one up, and serving. In terms of sheer quality of play, the fourth was maybe the best set we played in the final. Both of us were at the very top of our games, ending long rallies with one winner after another, making few errors. I was always a game ahead because I served first, so Federer was always serving to stay in the match, but he succeeded every time. Don't ever say Federer is not a fighter.

The set went to a tiebreak and it was me to serve first. The Centre Court crowd had by now lost all restraint, one half yelling "Roger! Roger!"; the other, "Rafa! Rafa!" On the first point, for once, I went up to the net, instantly receiving a reminder of why I do it so rarely. Federer passed me comfortably down the forehand side. A bad start. But then I went on an amazing streak. Confident, master of my game, I won both points on his serve. Then, handing Federer some of his own medicine, I served an ace, followed by another good first serve he could not return. I was up 4–1. If I held my remaining serves, I'd be Wimbledon champion. I didn't dare imagine victory yet, though all my shots were coming off. But I wasn't pumping my fists, as in similar circumstances elsewhere I usually would; I was very deliberately keeping myself as cool and focused as I could, trying to give an impression of nervelessness, remembering all the time this was Federer, a tennis player more equipped to pull something out of nothing than anyone alive.

He was serving now, and I was more relaxed than I knew I would be on my next serve because I'd broken him twice and was ahead. If I grabbed a point on his serve, it would be an unexpected plus. But I was not depending on this. I didn't have the same pressure as he did to win the next two points, and that gave me a momentary respite, until my turn came to serve. I told myself: "Stick to the game plan, keep hitting high topspins to his backhand." But he worked around the backhand on the next point, winning it with an electric forehand down the line.

We changed sides with me 4–2 up. I took my customary sip of water from each of my two bottles; he walked back on court. I jumped up after him and ran to receive. The next rally was nervy and long, fifteen shots, both of us playing cautiously, me containing what might have been the suicidal urge to finish things off with a winning drive, and the point ending with him losing his nerve first and hitting a backhand well wide. I allowed myself a moment of celebration: a discreet, controlled, slow-motion punch. Nothing too exuberant, nothing the crowd on the Centre Court could see, but inside—I couldn't help myself—I felt this was nearly, nearly it. Serving, at 5–2 up, I felt I was within touching distance of my life's dream. And that was my downfall.

Until now, the adrenaline had beaten the nerves; now suddenly the nerves trumped all. I felt as if I were on the edge of a precipice. As I bounced the ball up and down before my first serve, I thought, "Where should I hit it? Should I be brave and aim at his body, trying to catch him by surprise, even though I failed with that gambit a couple of sets back?" I shouldn't have given it so much thought. I should have served wide to his backhand, as I had been doing all the way through. But I aimed straight and hard and hit it long. Now I was very, very nervous. I had entered unknown territory, never having felt sensations quite like this before. As I tossed the ball up, I said to myself, "Double fault danger: don't blow it." But I knew I'd blow it. I was so, so tight. And, yes, I hit the second serve, tamely, into the net. The nerves were eating me up. But it wasn't the fear of losing that was causing it; it was the fear of winning. I wanted to win Wimbledon so desperately badly, I longed to win this match and had longed for this moment all my life: this was the great core truth that I had striven to keep hidden from myself by seeking to concentrate on the match one point at a time, never looking back or looking forward. But the temptation to look forward proved too great; my excitement on the brink of victory betrayed me.

What the fear of winning means is that, while you know what shot you have to play, the legs and the head do not respond. The nerves take possession of them and you can't hold on; you can't endure. It wasn't fear of losing, because at no point in the match did I feel I wasn't capable of winning. I never lost heart. From start to finish I felt I deserved not to lose, that I was doing everything right and that I had prepared myself in the best possible way before the match had begun.

But as I stood poised to serve again at 5–3, the conviction had gone. I lost my courage. Because instead of carrying on playing, putting that setback of the double fault immediately out of my mind, I let it influence my next serve. I was thinking, "Whatever you do, get the first serve in. Don't risk a second double fault. Just get the first one in, any way you can!" And I did, but it was a weak serve, a cautious second serve masquerading as a first serve, a coward's serve. Yes, that is the right word. It was a moment of cowardliness. And it allowed him immediately to go on the attack. He hit his return deep, I returned the shot short, he hit deep again, and I failed—abysmally—on the backhand return, hitting the ball lame and low into the net. It was a far from impossible shot to get back; nine times out of ten there would have been no problem. I might even have hit a winner from it. But my arm had tightened, my rhythm was shot, my body out of position. Instead of leaning with conviction into the stroke, my legs had been all over the place, a mangle of twisted nerves.

It was 5–4, his service. The initiative had shifted to Federer. He delivered a great first serve, wide to my forehand. I clawed it back, short, and he put away a winner. I was thinking, "I've screwed up. But it's 5–5 and I'm still in the tiebreak. If I win a point, this point, I'll have a match point to be champion of Wimbledon. I'm thinking, 'What a screwup, but I'll go for this point.'" But he banged down another great serve and I was almost done for. Now it was he who was on set point, with me serving. Suddenly, I was not as nervous as I had been; not as worried about doing a double fault. I'd backed off the precipice. The fear of winning had gone, and I was in a situation that was less comfortable but to which I was more accustomed: battling to save the set. I hit my first serve into the net, but now I was no longer thinking "double fault." I hit a decent second serve, and a long rally began, with me pummeling his backhand. I hit the ball wide to his forehand but a little short, and there he had his chance. He went for a winning drive and it went wide.

We changed sides again. As always, Federer resumed his position before I did. I had to towel myself down, take my two swigs from my two bottles of water. Then I trotted back to take up my position to serve. I struck a good first serve at last, initiating a strong rally in which we both hit the ball hard and deep—in his case, finally, a little too deep. The ball was called long, but he challenged it. The image on the screen showed that the line judge had been right. It had been a moment of desperation from Federer, but I understood it. I'd have done the same at such a critical moment. I now had match point, on his serve. But he responded like the great champion he is, blasting down another of his unstoppable serves.

Just in case, more in hope than expectation, I looked at the umpire and issued a challenge of my own. It went his way. The ball had landed square on the line. We were 7–7, and an incredible point followed. For me. He hit a deep second serve, we exchanged a couple of shots, he thundered a forehand wide and deep to my forehand, I ran across the back of the baseline, he rushed to the net, and I passed him low and straight down the line. An amazing shot.

I had another match point, and now I had conquered my nerves. I thought I deserved to be where I was and that I was on the brink of conquering Wimbledon. Dumb. Really dumb. It was one of the very, very few moments in my entire career in which I thought I'd won, before I'd won. The emotions got the better of me, and I forgot the golden rule in tennis, more than any other sport, that it's not over till it's over.

The score was 8–7 and I had match point on my serve. I did exactly what I had to do, served wide to his backhand. He hit it back short, mid-court, and, here, right here, was the very first moment in my entire life in which, approaching to hit the ball, before I'd made impact, I was filled with the euphoric sensation that victory was mine. I drove a forehand to his backhand corner and rushed the net, believing he was going to miss it or hit a weak reply that I'd easily put away. He didn't. He whistled a sensational backhand down the line and I didn't get close to it. I've replayed that point in my head many, many times. I have the tape of it in my head.

What might I have done differently? I could have hit the ball harder and deeper, or I could have hit it to his forehand side. But I don't think, even now, that hitting it to his forehand would have been the right thing to do. Here's why: if I'd hit it there and he'd passed me, or he'd got the ball back and I'd missed, I'd have been devastated. Because I'd have deviated from my plan to aim always at his backhand; I'd have known immediately that I had made the wrong choice. That would have affected me very badly mentally. As it was, I made the right choice, even if the execution had not been as effective as it might have been. It wasn't a bad shot, though. Often enough he'd have failed on that return. To be fair to myself, he did hit a really fantastic shot, and at a moment of unbelievable pressure for him. On the previous point I had hit my best shot of the match, and he had responded immediately with his best. Only later, when it was all over, was I able to reflect that it was because of moments like these, when the drama was at its highest, that this Wimbledon final had been so special.

That winner gave him a high. He ran me ragged on the next point, hitting with furious confidence, and won it with a cross-court forehand I couldn't touch. He served for the set at 9–8 in the tiebreak, hitting his first ball long, prompting a large part of the crowd to respond with a very unusual "Aaah!" of disappointment. The crowd didn't want the match to end. They wanted a fifth set. And that was what they got. I hit my return long on his second serve, and now it really was back to square one. Two sets all—for all practical purposes, love-all in the match.

MALLORCANS

IT WAS NO surprise when Sebastián Nadal and his wife, Ana María, rejected the apparently inviting offer their son received during his teens to take up a tennis scholarship in Barcelona. And it was even less of a surprise that he should have responded to his parents' decision with relief. The island exercises a powerful pull over Rafa Nadal: he always misses home when he is away competing in international tournaments; he always rushes back at the earliest possible opportunity, by the fastest available means.

It says much about his competitive grit, and something about the gap between his sporting and his private personas, that he only feels fully himself when he is at home. Nadal the tennis player triumphs on tennis courts everywhere; outside Mallorca, Nadal the man is like a fish out of water.

The reasons why have to do with the strong sense of identity that characterizes the islanders, but also with the fact that Mallorca is the one place in the world where he can feel normal, where the nature of the inhabitants is such that they relate to him as he thinks people should: not on account of what he has achieved, but by virtue of who he is.

The Nadals take pride in the belief that they define, and are defined by, Mallorcan culture, nowhere more manifestly so than in the diamond-hard tightness of their family ties, the foundation on which Rafa's drive and mental resilience are built. The strength of the family bond in Mallorca is unusual even in the context of a country as rooted in Catholic tradition as Spain. Another characteristic of the Spanish is their loyalty and sense of belonging to the town or village of their forebears. But in this instance, too, the Mallorcans take things a step further, all the more so in the case of the Nadals, who keep their closest relationships within their home town of Manacor, the island's third biggest town.

Sebastián and Ana María were born and raised there, as were their parents, and their parents' parents; so too were Rafa and his girlfriend of more than five years, María Francisca. So intimately does Rafa identify with his birthplace that it is hard to imagine him having a relationship with a woman from anywhere else. His natural habitat is Manacor, and for him to be sentimentally involved with someone from Miami or Monte Carlo would seem almost as unnatural as the crossing of two different species.

Rafa's extended family, stretching three generations, all live in Manacor or in the town's satellite beach resort of Porto Cristo. And Rafa's closest male friends are almost all Manacor natives too, not least among them Rafael Maymó, his physical therapist. Two intimates from out of town, Carlos Moyá and his physical trainer Joan Forcades, were born close by in Palma, the capital of Mallorca.

As for the presence of two Catalans, Carlos Costa and Jordi Robert, on Nadal's globe-trotting professional team, that has an explanation too. For Mallorcans there are two classes of "foreigners": Catalans and the rest. The proximity of language and geography (the Catalan capital of Barcelona is barely half an hour away by plane) grants the Catalans the status of first cousins. Benito Pérez Barbadillo, who is Spanish but from Andalucía, is valued and viewed affectionately within Nadal's team, but he operates by different codes, is decidedly extroverted—as Andalucians tend to be—and is thus regarded, from an amused and mildly perplexed distance, as the odd one out.

The impulse Mallorcans have to stick together has encouraged the view among visitors from the rest of Spain that the islanders are a deeply "mistrustful" people. A quick look at the history of the island helps explains why such a perception might not be off the mark. Mallorca, a tiny speck on the map of Europe, has been a target for foreign invaders and occupiers for at least two thousand years. First it was the Romans, then the Vandals, then the Moors, then the Spanish and, in a tourism boom that started fifty years ago, British and German visitors—"barbarians from the north," in local parlance—many of whom have stayed and colonized the more picturesque parts of the island. (The permanent population of Mallorca stands at around 800,000; a parallel world of 12 million tourists passes through the island each year.)

All along, and in between, pirates have plundered Mallorca's coasts. Which might account for why it was apparently not uncommon halfway through the last century to come across Mallorcan country folk who had never thought to venture near the sea—or who had never even seen it—or who would ask, "What's bigger, Mallorca, or beyond Mallorca?" Their longstanding response to coexisting with foreign occupiers has been a quiet, prudent passivity.

Sebastián Nadal, who does not dispute this impression, urges outsiders keen to understand the culture of his birthplace to read a little book, popular on the island among natives and visitors alike, called *Dear Mallorcans.* Its pages reinforce, if anything, the notions held by other Spaniards of the islanders, describing them as "phlegmatic" and "always ready to listen but not always to speak." That corresponds to the character of Sebastián Nadal and his son; but it does not mesh with the talkative Toni, which maybe helps account for the perception within his family that he is something of a misfit.

Yet if Rafa Nadal has conquered the tennis world and become a name known on every continent, it is because in some important respects he, like Toni, has defied the stereotypes that define the islanders. "In Mallorca, people seek success more in the pleasure of living than in work and they have a concept of time tied more to leisurely enjoyment than to the material results of effort," *Dear Mallorcans* informs us. In his unusual embrace of the Protestant work ethic, Rafa Nadal has more in common with the recent German colonizers than with the ancestral natives of Mallorca. Carlos Moyá, also from Mallorca and also a tennis champion, but by his own admission an infinitely less ambitious one than Nadal, makes the point that the lust to triumph both Rafa and Toni exhibit bears no relation to a Mallorcan character he describes as "relaxed, almost Caribbean."

Beyond tennis, on the other hand, Rafa Nadal does share what the island bible describes as the Mallorcans' peculiarly lackadaisical attitude toward time. He is not punctual by nature, and if he is enjoying himself with his friends back home, he will not think twice about staying up clubbing until five in the morning. The difference between him and his friends is that, breaking with island convention, he will then unfailingly wake up four hours later and go to the tennis court to train. When the sport to which he has dedicated his life makes its call, he ceases to be a hedonist son of the Mediterranean and becomes a model of disciplined self-denial.

His fellow Mallorcans respect him for the deviant path he has chosen, and for the success he has brought to the island, but they refuse to be impressed. "Mallorca is a not a place that produces too many heroes," *Dear Mallorcans* says, "but those it does are not feted in the least." The truth of this is the reason why Manacor is the only place on the planet where Rafa Nadal can stroll down the street in broad daylight or walk into a shop safe in the knowledge that he will not be assailed for a signature or a photograph, not mobbed by strangers on the streets. It is another example of the islanders' habitual reserve. Self-display of any kind is frowned upon ("Who does he think he is?" would be the reaction if Rafa's success had led him to assume new airs and graces), and by the same rule, showering praise on people, however much deserved the praise might be, is considered in bad taste. "Anyone who tries to raise their head above the rest," *Dear Mallorcans* tells us, "will immediately have it chopped off." When Nadal is not playing tennis he has no desire to raise his head above the rest—quite the opposite, in fact. That is why, as Nadal's mother, Ana María, says, Mallorca is the only place where he can disconnect completely. "If he weren't able to keep coming back after tournaments, he would go mad," she says. For Rafa Nadal, whose tennis life is a frenzy, the return home to Mallorca signifies peace.

CHAPTER 6

"AN INVASION OF THE PUREST JOY"

THERE ARE MATCHES in which, come the final set, I still have something in reserve. I feel my game can still go up a gear. Not this time. Not at the start of the fifth at Wimbledon. I was playing as well as I knew how, yet I had lost each of the last two sets on a tiebreak to Federer. The danger now was to let it get to me, to lose heart. Federer was doing to me what I often did to other players. He had salvaged a very tough situation; he was fighting back from difficult odds, winning the most critical points. I had just thrown away a big chance to win. To complicate things further, he was serving first. That was an advantage in the decisive set because the chances were that I'd have to hold each one of my service games in order to remain in the match. Neither of us had broken the other's serve in twenty-five games, and with both of us playing our best tennis, an early break by me did not feel too likely. But I was thinking straight. I was burning on the outside, but inside I was cold. As I sat in my chair waiting for the set to begin, I wasn't lamenting the loss of the last two sets, I wasn't letting my failure to capitalize on the 5–2 advantage I had on the last tiebreak eat me up. The double fault was gone, forgotten. I was thinking pragmatically, the way my father does under pressure. Enduring means accepting. Accepting things as they are and not as you would wish them to be, and then looking ahead, not behind. Which means taking stock of where you are and thinking coolly. I was telling myself: "Don't worry about breaking his serve in the first game, focus on winning your own in the second one." If not, if I made one mistake on my serve on the wrong point, he'd be 3–love up and there, mentally, I'd be on the rack. I'd see victory very far away, even if it was just the one break he'd made. I had to win my first service game and the next two, that was the priority now. Because he was coming from a very positive dynamic and he was at his most dangerous. But I knew what I had to do: if I managed to hold on to those first three service games, we'd be at 3–3 and I'd have halted his momentum. He wouldn't have a following wind anymore, and we'd be back to all square in the mental game we were both playing, hidden to the crowd. The smallest error on his part, and again I'd be on the brink of winning; the smallest error by me, and he'd have victory in his hands. I wanted to make sure that I kept holding my serve until we reached that stage of the match when everything would be up for grabs.

Losing to Federer in five sets the previous year at Wimbledon, after losing four break points in the final set, had haunted me, but this was the moment in the match when that experience of defeat proved most valuable. I had been very close to winning back then; I knew I could have, but the reason I didn't win was that on too many points my emotions had gotten the better of my reason. I hadn't been prepared to cope with the inevitable nerves and tension with the due measure of mental calm.

I'd need that now because this was going to be what in Spain we'd call a "heart attack" set. I could tell from the glances I shot my family that they were frozen with fear, remembering 2007. I was remembering that too, but in a constructive light now. I had learned my lesson and felt capable of putting it into practice. I began the fifth set feeling lithe and loose, believing I was going to win. Blowing my chance in the fourth had made me stronger, not weaker. Because I wasn't going to buckle again the way I had then. I wasn't going to serve another weak double fault. I was going to think not of winning the game, but of winning the point. I was going to let instinct take over, let the thousands of hours of accumulated practice kick naturally into play.

Two years earlier, after I'd beaten Federer at the French Open and lost to him in the first of our three Wimbledon finals, I had thought that there was more chance of him completing his Grand Slam foursome with a victory at Roland Garros than of me ever triumphing here in the Centre Court. Since 2006, I'd stayed at number two in the world rankings, giving him chase, but never quite getting close enough. It had been a time more of keeping pace than of dramatic leaps forward. I had great runs on clay again in 2007 and 2008, winning the French Open for a third and fourth time, establishing my authority over the competition in much the same way Federer had established his over Wimbledon. It was particularly satisfying to establish a record at Monte Carlo, my home away from home, to become, in 2008, the first professional player to win that tournament four times in a row. I beat Federer 7–5, 7–5 in the final, and immediately I felt a strong urge to get back home as soon as possible. I didn't want to spend another night in Monte Carlo, however much I liked the place; I wanted to get back home straightaway, and the only way to do it was to catch a budget flight to Barcelona and from there connect to Palma. I remember the look of surprise on the other passengers' faces at Nice airport as I joined them in the departure lounge to board the orange easyJet airplane. They were surprised to see me queuing up with the rest of them to buy a drink and a sandwich. One asked me why I didn't fly on a private jet. The truth is I don't like it. I could push one of my sponsors to fly me around, but I wouldn't feel comfortable doing that. It's a bit too flashy for me, and besides, I don't like abusing my relationship with them. But when we had boarded and I struggled to fit the squat, wide Monte Carlo cup into the luggage compartment above my seat, I did for a second wonder whether I'd made the right choice There was an uproar in the flight cabin, laughter and clapping, as I tried from every angle to wedge the trophy into place. Another passenger on the flight asked me whether there were any serious rivals for me out there, beyond Federer. I didn't hesitate to reply. "Novak Djokovic," I said. "He'll be challenging us hard in a couple of years' time."

Already he had been giving me trouble. While I had beaten him in Indian Wells in 2007, to win my first tournament on U.S. soil, I lost to him in the following tournament, the Miami Masters. I won playing him in the French Open semis and in the Wimbledon semis that year too, then lost to him in the Canadian Masters, which he won. When we faced off again a year later, in 2008, I lost to him at Indian Wells, before going on to beat him in Hamburg and in the French Open. But he'd already won a Grand Slam in January that year, the Australian Open, at the age of twenty. Everybody still had their eyes on Federer and me, but we both knew Djokovic was the up-and-coming star and that our dual dominance was going to be more at risk from him than from any other player. Disconcertingly, he was also younger than me. This was something new. I had been accustomed all my life until this point, in tennis and also in the junior football leagues of Mallorca, to being the young kid who had the audacity to take on and beat his elders. This younger guy was now beating me, and even when I won, he was giving me very tough games. Federer would presumably retire before I did, assuming injury didn't do me in. Djokovic would be dogging me right to the end of my career, trying everything to jump ahead of me in the rankings.

On clay I had an edge over him, as I did over Federer and everybody else. But on hard courts I struggled against him, as I did against many others. That was the surface I had to work hardest on to adjust. I was failing to make the leap I needed to make on the faster surfaces, so far making little headway in Australia and less in what seemed to be the most difficult Grand Slam tournament for me, the US Open. I'm never satisfied, I always want more. Or, at any rate, I want to push myself to the very limit of my abilities.

Meanwhile, I was making more money than I'd ever imagined, though the thought never even crossed my mind of buying myself an apartment in Monte Carlo, or Miami, or even Mallorca. I was more than happy to continue living at my parents' home. But this was not a question of being frugal. I dreamed of buying myself a boat and anchoring it at Porto Cristo. I had the occasional notion of buying myself a fancy car, a fantasy that took shape one June day during the 2008 French Open.

I was strolling around with my father when we passed a luxury sports car store. I stopped, looked in the window, saw this beautiful vehicle, and said to my father, "You know what? I think I might like to buy myself one of those." My father looked at me as if I was nuts. I understood his reaction. I had expected it. There's nothing written on the subject, no law against it, but I knew as well as he that owning such a car might be interpreted by the rest of the family and by our neighbors in Manacor—and, indeed, by my father himself—as a vulgarly ostentatious extravagance. I felt a bit sheepish. But, in my heart of hearts, I still wanted that car. If my father had said no, no way, I would have given up on the idea at once. I wouldn't have gone ahead and bought the car without his blessing. But, instead, he came up with what he thought was a devious compromise. He said, "Look, if you win Wimbledon this year, you can buy yourself one of those. How about that?" I said, "How about if I win the French Open here in Paris this week?" He smiled and said, "No, no. You win Wimbledon, then you can buy it." He had replied, as I knew perfectly well at the time, with the mischievous conviction that Wimbledon was not within my reach that year. He never thought he'd lose that bet. A month later, at the start of the final set on Wimbledon's Centre Court, it was yet one more incentive for me to beat Federer and win the Grand Slam tournament all players most cherished.

Calm as I thought I was, given that the nerves were obviously there, I did not cover myself in glory on the very first point, on Federer's serve. After a sharp exchange of shots, I forced him into a fluffed backhand that just made it over the net off the frame of his racket. Instead of going for the winner, I opted for a drop shot. You try a drop when there is no alternative, the ball landing too far away from you to do otherwise, or when you see that your opponent has been driven deep and will have little chance of reaching it. But sometimes you do it because the nerves get to you, the ball feels a little too hot to handle and you don't dare hit it hard. That was what I did. There was a little bit of cowardice behind that shot. He got to it sharply enough, lobbed me on the backhand side, I strained up to reach it, and I hit it wide. A bad start.

It was important not to reinforce what might have been the gathering impression in Federer's mind that I was weakening, that I was going to keep on missing the chances that came my way. So

I thought, "You're feeling good despite that momentary loss of nerve; next chance you get, next half chance, go for a hard return." That was exactly what I did on his wide second serve. I lashed back a cross-court forehand, way beyond his reach. I actually didn't mean to hit it quite so well, so close to the line, but no complaints about the outcome.

He won the next point on a powerful serve, and then he succumbed to exactly the same loss of nerve as I had on the first point. He delivered another strong first serve that I returned weakly, but instead of thumping it away, he tried a drop. Except that this time it didn't even make it over the net. Having aimed at this stage of the set merely to hold serve, I saw an unexpected opportunity suddenly loom at 30–all, but he got two powerful first services in and the game was his. Then I lost the first point on my first service game, hitting a forehand just wide. It's never good to go love–15 down on your serve, but it was even less so now, when every single point was critical; I was fighting to hold my serve, and the crowd, whose energy levels only grew the longer the match went on, knew it. I stayed composed and poker faced. I won the next point, and then Federer let slip to me how anxious he had become when he issued a challenge on a high topspin forehand of mine that landed square on the line. Our game was not on the same level as it had been in the fourth set. We were sounding each other out nervily. The difference between us was that my first serves were not going in, while his were, but, after mistakes on both sides, I won the game at 30. I made my right hand into a fist. I glanced up at my sister and my uncles and aunt. They nodded encouragement. Serious nods. Some of the other fans might be smiling; not my family.

Federer served at 1–1, his first serve reliably going in every single time, it seemed. But that was the only part of his game that was working well. Whenever I managed to gain just a little of the initiative, he was missing simple shots. Then, very unexpectedly, he double faulted, bringing the game to deuce. Neither of us was at his best, but I was playing less badly. He seemed to have lost the winning momentum of the fourth set. The tide was inching slightly toward me. Then I hit a forehand needlessly long and shook my head. I didn't shout with rage, which was what I felt like doing, but I was upset with myself for gifting him a point when all the pressure should have been on him. On the next point I played another drop, but this time an attacking one, which he was too good even for him to make an effort to reach. But then he won the next two points and the game.

Once again I had to hold my serve to stop him pulling away. But I was quietly growing in confidence, sensing that the huge effort he'd made in coming back from two sets down was beginning to sap his energy. We'd have to see whether he would be able to sustain the level he'd shown in the third and fourth sets, each of which he'd won by the very tightest of margins. That was maybe an optimistic interpretation of how things were right then, but the alternative, to allow negative thoughts to enter my head, would have been suicide.

I held my serve comfortably, far more so than he had held his the game before, thanks in part to an awful error on his part. I hit a poor drop shot once again—my mind seized up for a split second—but he, going for what was a clear chance of a winner, mishit the ball horribly long, the way an ordinary club player might. It was not all pretty at this stage of the match, but we were 2–2 and I had won several more points in the set so far than he had, which counted for nothing in the score, but placed more of a weight on his mind than mine.

The wind picked up; I looked up at the sky. It was darkening fast and it was getting harder for the line judges to do their job. We made a challenge each in the fifth game, on his serve, and both went my way. The score reached deuce, and then the rain came. Federer signaled he wanted to go off, and the umpire agreed. This was not, on the face of it, good news for me. I had been in the lead by two sets when the first rain break came, and then he had come back to win the next two; both of us were playing more poorly at the start of the fifth than at any point in the match, but he was playing more poorly than I was, his serve proving to be his best, and almost only, weapon. And, despite that, I was not the one who had been struggling to hold my serve, he was. I think I was in better shape, and on balance, it would have been best for me not to stop now. He needed a breather more badly than I did.

That was also what Toni seemed to be thinking, judging from his appearance when he and Titín joined me in the dressing room. And, as I found out when we talked about the game much later, that was certainly what was on the minds of the rest of the family, who felt the fates were conspiring against me. My father said the two rain interruptions, but in particular the second one, had been pure torture for him. Logic told him that it would have suited me more for the game to continue, because he felt it cost me more to get back my rhythm than Federer. "In my mind, the rain meant you were condemned to lose," my father confessed later. As for my mother, she could see I was playing better than Federer at that moment, and she was sure that the rain, interrupting as it was my momentum, acted in Federer's favor. The rest of the family there at the Centre Court all saw it the same way. Wondering what they might have done wrong in their lives to have to put up with so much torment, they could hardly bear to watch. And each of them thought, "If I'm feeling like this, how must Rafael be?"

Toni's face in the locker room showed the strain, Titín, who came in with him, was more impassive, giving nothing away, waiting for me to set the mood. He told me later he had been a nervous wreck but had disguised his feelings behind the mask of his professional duties, changing my bandages, taking a good look at my left foot, the troublesome one, which luckily remained numb, not bothering me at all. Titín put his head down and quietly got on with his tasks. Toni's job was, as it had been all our lives, to find the right words for the occasion. But he was struggling this time. He later admitted that after the rain came in that fifth set he had resigned himself to me losing. He tried to put a brave face on it, tried to suppress what he was really feeling, and began a little speech that I'd heard before and which, I could tell, his heart was not really in. As I sat on the bench, he stood over me and said, "Look, however small the possibility might be of victory, fight to the very end. The reward is too great for you not to make the effort. So many times, due to dismay or exhaustion, players don't put up the battle circumstances demand, but if there is one chance, just one, you must fight on until all is lost. If you can get to 4–4, it won't be the best player who'll win, it'll be the one who has better control of his nerves."

Toni had obviously entered the locker room supposing that I would be devastated by the opportunities I had lost in the third and fourth sets, imagining that I had convinced myself they would not come back again, and that therefore he now faced the mission impossible of trying to lift my crushed spirits. He'd misread me. He was operating on the previous year's script, obviously as haunted as the rest of the family was by the state I'd been in after I lost. I was operating on a different script. He was surprised by my reply. "Relax. Don't worry.

I'm calm. I can do it. I'm not going to lose." Toni was taken aback, did not know what to say. "Well," I continued, "maybe he ends up winning it, but I won't lose as I did last year." I meant that, whatever happened, I wasn't going to hand him victory on a plate. I wasn't going to lower my guard and I wasn't going to let myself down. He was going to have to fight every inch of the way too, and I would not be ceding any ground. This time in the locker room, by contrast to what had happened during the first rain interruption, it was Federer who was quiet, I who was chattering. Once Toni recovered from the surprise of seeing that he had no need to buck me up, we talked about the game in more clinical terms. I mentioned a couple of the errors I'd made in the fourth set, but not to beat myself up. I thought that by speaking about them I'd make sure I remembered those lapses and did not repeat them again. I recalled my failures in the tiebreak of the fourth when I went 5–2 up and my two missed match points, not so much as opportunities missed, as Toni saw them, but as evidence of how close I'd been to winning, of how up against the ropes I'd put Federer, of how—should those chances come again—I would not fail. Also, as I reminded Toni, I had not lost my serve once, while Federer had lost his twice, despite so far having served about five times as many aces as I had. And, besides, if I'd won two sets already, why shouldn't I win a third?

My father, my mother, everybody confessed later that when Toni got back from the locker room, they were amazed to hear from him how sunny and constructive my mood had been. Some of them wondered if I was just putting it on, either to deceive myself or to calm their nerves. Toni told them he'd wondered the same thing but had heard something in my tone of voice and seen something in my eyes that told him I was for real. I was. I knew this was my moment.

Titín knew it too. We've talked about that moment quite a few times since. He had expected something else, as Toni had, but discovered that now, in the last throes of the match, I looked more confident and more at ease than I had done the night before at dinner or when we'd been playing darts, or that morning during training, or over lunch. After half an hour, when the rain stopped, Titín left the locker room believing, as I did, that my time had finally come to win Wimbledon.

It was 2–2 and deuce, with Federer serving. He banged down two aces and won the game. Nothing I could do about that. Aces are like rain. You accept them and move on. I replied with a great forehand winner at the start of my service game, which I won at 15, and then he held serve easily at love, wrapping up the game with yet another ace. In the next game, with me serving at 4–3 down, he had his chance. He won the first point after I hit a forehand just wide. I challenged it, but more in hope than expectation. Love–15. We got to 30–30, and then, suddenly, he hit a perfect forehand winner down the line, wrong-footing me when I had expected the ball to come to my backhand, and I was 30–40 down. It was the first break point of the set and one of the biggest points of my life. I did not think of the consequences. I did not think that if I lost this one, he'd go 5–3 up and, the way he was serving, the match would surely be his. I just thought: "Concentrate every gram of energy and every cell in your brain and everything you've ever done in your life into holding this next point." I had the sense then that he was going to try and hit the ball hard, go for a quick winner, so I had to stop him from getting the opportunity to do so, and the way to do that was by going on the attack first. The moment had come to vary the game plan, take him by surprise, do the unexpected. Instead of angling the first serve wide to his backhand, as I was doing on 90 percent of my serves, I hit it straight at his body, forcing him into an awkward forehand return that arrived back mid-court. I knew he'd thought I'd drive the ball high to his backhand, but I surprised him again. This was no time for half measures. I had overcome my fears, and the moment had come to attack, and so I opened up my chest and drove a forehand deep and hard into his forehand corner. All he could do was stretch and reply with a lob that went into orbit but landed close to the net. I finished off the point pounding the ball hard into the grass and high up into the Centre Court seats. I pumped my fist. Never had I played a point so pressured so bravely, intelligently, and well. I won the next point and then the game, wrong-footing him with a clean, looping forehand winner to his backhand corner.

The score was 4–4. I was where I wanted to be; and now the moment had come to fight, play aggressively, go for broke on every point, wait for my chance to pounce. If you've made it to the fifth set of a match like this, it means you're playing well enough to risk going on the attack. Besides, there was no option now. Toni had said that if we got to 4–4, the winner would be the player better able to control his nerves. I felt I had control of mine. I also felt the Centre Court crowd was swinging toward me. In the previous set they'd been rooting more for Federer because they wanted the match to go to five sets, but now I heard more cries of "Rafa! Rafa!" than "Roger! Roger!" I like to have the crowd behind me, of course, but I savor it more after the game is over, or when I watch the match again on video, than at the time. When I am playing I cannot allow anything to distract me, not even the support of the fans.

Maybe they were with me because they thought I was playing better and deserved victory more. That was how I felt now as the match neared its close. He wasn't hitting the ball as cleanly as I was and was even mis-hitting some forehands, usually the strongest part of his game. I sensed I was winning the battle of nerves, and I also sensed he was more tired than I was. The difference remained that he had a weapon I lacked: the big serve. That kept getting him out of trouble, and that won him the next game, putting him 5–4 ahead. Now I was going to have to serve not just to avoid the break, but to save the match.

I couldn't match him for power on the service, but I could try and outwit him. I did, sending down an ace after going 15–0 up on the first point. I aced him not because I hit the ball hard but because he was expecting it on his backhand and I bent the ball wide to his right. I felt confident and I was letting him know it. I won the game, pretty comfortably, at 30. And then it was he who found himself in deep trouble. I went 15–40 up on his serve after hitting a curling forehand down the line from deep in the left-hand baseline corner. Two break points and I was flying, but then, bang! An ace. And then another big serve. He won the game to go up 6–5. My consolation was knowing that, unlike the time in the third set when I had lost a chance to break him at love–40, this had been no fault of my own. I had another kind of mental battle to contend with now, fighting my growing frustration at the mechanical effectiveness of his serve. I knew once a point got under way, I was getting the upper hand, but he just wasn't allowing me the chance to play my game.

Again I had to serve to save the match, and again I did it with relative ease, winning it at 15. Federer had little answer to my aggression once a rally got under way, though I'm not sure that was the way my father was seeing it at the time. I glanced up at him after I'd won that game to make it 6-6 and he was going berserk, on his feet, applauding, his face urging me on with rage and elation, contorted in a way I'd never seen it before. Going berserk was not an option for me right now. I had the feeling that if I kept my head, victory was mine. Federer's groundstrokes were falling apart. In the first point at 6–6—no tiebreak now as it was the final set—he mishit a simple forehand terribly. Then I won the next point after the first long rally on his serve that I could remember. Then three more pounding serves and he was up 40–30. I could see for sure now that he was more tired than I was and more uncertain of his shots, so I was getting more and more frustrated at the unflagging consistency of his serve, which was proving to be his only escape route. I thought, "I'm definitely playing better, but what more can I do . . . ?"

I leveled at deuce, and then I saw my chance when, at last, he missed his first serve. But no: I returned his second serve hard and long. About half a meter long. Now, that might have looked like a very poor mistake, but in a way it wasn't. Because it meant I remained committed to attack, that I was playing all-or-nothing tennis. If I'd lost the point hitting the ball short, into the net, that would have been a sign that my head was failing me. But that was a shot struck with conviction. Messing up is part of the game, but sometimes it's more productive to lose a point through an error of your own than because the other guy has hit a winner.

All points are important, but some are more important than others. Now every single one was worth gold. My uncle Rafael, who was there at the Centre Court, told me afterward that in my place he simply could not have withstood the pressure, that his legs would have given way, that he would simply have run off, got on a flight somewhere far away, and never come back. The difference between me and him, and other spectators who might have had similar thoughts, was that I had trained for this moment all my life. Not just hitting balls, but training my mind. Toni's harsh training regime—thwacking balls at me when I was a little kid to keep me alert, never allowing me to make excuses or succumb to complacency—was reaping its reward. Plus I do have a quality—whether innate or taught, I don't know—that champions must have: pressure elates me. Yes, I buckle sometimes, but more often I raise my game.

The whole story of my match so far had been one of missed opportunities. Not capitalizing on a love–40 on his serve to break him in the third set, missing two match points in the fourth, and now, in the fifth, not breaking him when I was 15–40 up on his serve at 5–5 or love–30 up at 6–6. Now he was 7–6 up, and yet again I was serving to save my life. But I was more thrilled than fearful. I'd missed opportunities, but they had been my opportunities. They were something to celebrate rather than to lament. And sooner or later—I forced myself to think—I'd take my chance.

But he won the first point. A good, long return of serve and then an unanswerable winner. Nothing for me to do or say there. He played a great point. On to the next one. I recovered quickly. He hit a forehand long; I hit a first serve to his body that he could do nothing about, and then a long rally, where I returned every shot he hit with interest, ended with him hitting tamely into the net. He had failed to get his legs into position for the shot; he was more tired than I was. Seeing that gave me strength. But not overconfidence. I might have thought, "I've got him now," but I didn't. I thought, "I'm still in this, I can win." But I also knew that if I lost the next point he'd be two points away from being Wimbledon champion. And I did lose the next point, after he got a lucky net cord.

Then, at 40–30, one of the very best points in the match. I served wide to his backhand; he returned deep and well to my forehand. I pinned him back but he hit a strong backhand cross-court, to which I responded with an equally strong forehand down the line. He only just made it across, leaving him with no option but to hit an awkward sliced forehand that sailed just over the net and short. I scooped up a topspin shot low and wide to his backhand, and all he could respond with was a lob that I should have put away on the smash, but he somehow got to it, delivering another high, slow but better lob that obliged me to retreat and hit another less winnable smash, a controlled one with spin—like a second serve—after it had bounced. He got that one back too, with a sliced backhand to mid-court; I advanced on the ball and hit it, with all my might on the forehand, and with all the heavy topspin I could muster for an un-reachable winner, deep to his right-hand corner. 7–7. It was my mo-ment of greatest euphoria in the match so far. I raised my left knee, punched the air, roared in triumph. I had a rush of energy, a new charge of confidence, and I thought, "Come on, now!"

The match was there for the taking. But I had no vision of vic-tory yet. I was still taking it one point at a time. "My rhythm's good, my mobility is good, and I'm playing with conviction": that was how I felt. And I felt that now, at 7–7, the time really had come to go for the match; the momentum was with me and I should seize my chance. This was a game I had to win.

On the first point of his serve I picked up where I'd left off on my own service game, winning the rally on a cross-court forehand winner at which he could only flail. Then he messed up a forehand, into the net, and I was up love–30. Another big opportunity. But I am not a machine, I am not a locomotive. And on the next point I made a silly mistake. I opted for a backhand slice when I should have gone for a drive. For that split second, of all the split seconds, a tiny doubt entered my head, and I lost the point. Fear of winning. But not as serious as last time. My legs were not shaking. They felt strong.

I returned his next serve deep and won the point with a flashing cross-court backhand winner. I rolled my wrists, steering the ball with my right hand, powering it with my left arm—a shot I'd practiced all my life and that, when the moment of truth came, I hit as perfectly as I ever had. Two break points now, and my biggest fear was not that I'd fail but that he'd start pulling more of those big serves out of the hat. He did. An ace. Then another big serve. I slipped on the grass, lost my coordination; we were back to deuce.

I'd been here before. Over and over. This game was turning out to be a version in miniature of the whole match. Me pulling ahead; he, fighting back and back, refusing to go down. But he was still making more mistakes than I was, as he did on the next point, hitting a forehand out, very long, to give me advantage point. We were both at the outer edge of our capacity to endure, but, physically and mentally, he was more drained than I was. But he still had his serve, and bang came another unstoppable one that I could only flap at with the frame of my racket. But the moment I made a decent return of serve and the rally was on, it was me who got the upper hand. I won the next two points on two mistakes he made, two unforced errors on his forehand, one too short, one too long.

And here it was: a break of service at last. The score was 8–7 and I was serving for the match. It was after nine at night and it was getting dark fast. If we were back level after this game, the umpire might very well postpone the match to the next day. Such an interruption now, after four and three quarter hours of play, could only help Federer. I hadn't realized that as clearly when rain had come down earlier, but now there was no doubt he needed a respite more than I did. I thought, "I have to win this game by whatever means."

I ran to take up my position on the baseline, Federer walked to his. I was serving from the end where my parents were sitting, and they each stood up to give me a frenzied thumbs-up. But I lost the first point, a needlessly long forehand. The instant I prepared to hit the shot, I could see I was going to miss it, the mind clouded by nerves. I had to conquer those nerves right now, and the way to do it was to raise my aggression a notch. I had to beat myself before I could beat Federer. For the first time in the entire match I followed my serve up to the net, and it worked. I punched his return away for a winner. I hadn't planned it before I hit the serve, but it turned out to be the right spur-of-the-moment choice. If I'd let the ball bounce before hitting, the point would have remained open. The score was 15–15.

I won the next point at the net too, going in for the kill, an easy kill head high on the forehand volley, after forcing Federer wide and deep on his backhand. Again, it was a spontaneous decision to rush the net, the fruit of my determination to seize the game and not let the game seize me. 30–15 now, but I still wasn't seeing the finish line. Only the next point existed. Going to the net was a calculated risk in the growing darkness, and this time my calculation was wrong. So much so that I stuck my racket out at a forehand from Federer that, had I left it, would have gone well long, and I'd have had two match points. But I'd lost the point bravely, and that was better than losing on a double fault, or on a craven backhand slice.

30–30. "I'm still here," I thought. Reverting to my game plan, I attacked his backhand on the next rally and—maybe it was the light, or the exhaustion, or the nerves—he mishit a cross-court shot, sending it wide.

40–30 and match point, my third one of the match. I stuck to the safe and trusted option, a wide first serve to his backhand, which he returned with stunning brilliance and courage, with a cross-court thunderbolt that I strained but failed to reach. This was Roger Federer, the greatest player of all time, and this was why, even now, no thought of victory, no suggestion of complacency, was allowed. We were back to deuce.

Here I had the brilliant idea—it was, in retrospect, quite brilliant—of hitting my first serve wide to his forehand, when he had to be expecting that at a clutch moment like this I'd stick to the backhand route I'd been following practically the whole match. I managed to do, finally, what he'd been doing to me all match, curving down an unreturnable first serve. Not quite an ace, for he touched it with the end of his racket, but as good as. I had my fourth match point.

I hesitated on the serve. I should have gone for the backhand corner again, but I still registered in some corner of my mind that amazing backhand return of his on my previous match point, and so I aimed for the body instead. The serve ended up being neither one thing nor the other, and he might well have hit it for another winner, this time on the forehand, or put me under serious pressure at least. He did neither, returning the ball with little bite, giving me a simple forehand return that I hit with less conviction than I should have. He advanced on the ball, which dropped gently mid-court, and he hooked it, not for a winner, but badly, awkwardly, feet out of position, into the middle of the net.

I collapsed flat on my back on the Wimbledon grass, arms outstretched, fists clenched, roaring with triumph. The silence of the Centre Court gave way to pandemonium, and I succumbed, at long last, to the crowd's euphoria, letting it wash over me, liberating myself from the mental prison I had inhabited from start to finish of the match, all day, the night before, the full two weeks of the greatest tennis tournament on earth. Which I had finally won, at the third attempt: the consummation of my life's work, sacrifice, and dreams. The fear of losing, the fear of winning, the frustrations, the disappointments, the poor decisions, the moments of cowardice, the dread of ending up weeping once again on the floor of the locker room shower: all gone now. It wasn't relief I felt; I was beyond that. It was a rush of power and elation, an uncorking of emotion I had kept bottled up for the tensest four hours and forty-eight minutes of my life, an invasion of the purest joy.

Yet somehow I had to contain myself. I had to go up to the net to shake hands with Roger, from whom, after four years of waiting, I was about to take the number one spot in the world rankings, and the stiff formalities of the trophy presentation ceremony still beckoned. But the tears came, and there was nothing I could do to stop them, and there was one more thing I had to do before the ceremony, one emotional release I needed before I could behave with some semblance of the restraint that Wimbledon tradition required. I ran toward the corner where my father and mother and Toni, Titín, Carlos Costa, Tuts, and Dr. Cotorro had been sitting, and were now standing, and I clambered up the seats and scaled a wall to reach them. I was crying, and my father, the first to greet me, was crying too, and we hugged, and I hugged my mother, and I hugged Toni and the three of us all held one another in one great, tight family embrace.

Was that the greatest moment of my career? Every match is important; I play every one as if it is my last, but that one, in that setting, with that history, that expectation, that tension, the rain interruptions, the darkness, the number one against the number two, both of us playing at the top of our games, the comeback by Federer

and my resistance to it, me prouder than I ever had been of my attitude on a tennis court, haunted by the recollection of defeat in 2007
but fighting and winning my own war of nerves . . . so, yes, put it all
together, and it's almost impossible to imagine any other match that
could have generated so much drama and emotion and, for me, and
for those closest to me, such enormous satisfaction and joy.

THE LONGEST DAY

THE 2008 WIMBLEDON final between Rafa Nadal and Roger Federer was the longest in the tournament's 131-year history and, for many, the greatest tennis match there had ever been. John McEnroe, at the Centre Court commentating for American television, said it had been the best he'd seen. Björn Borg, who had also been ringside, but as a spectator, and who had defeated McEnroe in the greatest Wimbledon duel anyone could remember before this one, agreed that Nadal and Federer had served up the best match in history. Some members of the world's sports press suggested it had been the finest contest in any sport, period. The *New York Times* felt the match had been so unique it merited an editorial all of its own.

"The light slips away and though everyone feels the cumulative weight of what has come before, the players are still having to play in the present," the *Times* editorial said with uncanny insight, "still having to set aside the past in order to return another serve, while everyone in the crowd wonders how they do it—not just the imagination of the ball-striking, but the ability not to imagine, not to leap forward in their minds to winning or losing. Their desire is concealed in the play itself. But ours has gotten loose and is making it hard to breathe—hard even to watch."

If the *Times* editorial writer had found it hard to breathe, it is a wonder the Nadal family didn't die of collective asphyxia. "When it was over, I wept tears of elation," said Sebastián Nadal, after his longest day was finally over, "but I also had this sensation that my body had suddenly grown lighter, as if a huge weight had been lifted from my back. I had spent the whole match tortured by that awful fear that it would be 2007 all over again, that he would end up in tears in the shower and I would be able to do nothing to ease his grief.

"It was Tyson versus Holyfield out there, and I felt as if I'd been in the ring with them, exhausted, as if I'd suffered a terrible beating. People said my face changed during that match, that when they saw me on TV they couldn't recognize me. It was pure suffering, all the way through."

Toni Nadal knew Rafa the tennis player better than anyone, but even he had been staggered by the depths of resilience his nephew had showed. "Wimbledon had always been our dream, but in my heart of hearts I always feared it was an impossible dream," Toni said. "I had always pushed him to set his sights higher and higher, but I did not honestly believe he could climb this high. When he won, it was the first time I had ever cried on a tennis court."

Nadal's mother, Ana María, said the match had left her, as the Spanish expression goes, reduced to dust. "During the match there were moments when I just wanted it to stop. I thought, 'Leave it. Why does it have to matter so much whether you win or lose?' I kept asking myself how he could bottle up all that tension so tightly. Where does he get it from, my own son? How does he manage to stop falling apart?"

Carlos Moyá believes that, under such pressure, he himself would most definitely have fallen apart. "Just about any other player in history against Federer, playing with the courage and brilliance that he was, would have lost that match. When you've been so, so close and yet you haven't won, when you get to a fifth set, which basically means starting the match all over again, after having had victory in your hands, the emotions—if you are a normal player, or even a normal champion—just have to run away with you. You remember every missed chance, and those memories eat you up, devour your game. But not in Rafa's case. That's why he is no ordinary champion. Everything favored Federer at the start of the fifth, yet Rafa dominated him, tamed him, outplayed him."

Nadal, for Moyá that day, was a creature that refused to die. "Federer learned in that final that to beat Rafa you have to stomp on him not once, not twice, but many, many times. You think he's dead, in a point or in a game or in a set, but he keeps on coming back. That is why I think he can go on to beat all the records, why I think that, if he stays fit, he is capable of winning more Grand Slams than anyone ever has before."

Federer—world number one just for another three weeks, after which Nadal would snatch the title away from him—was shattered in defeat. "Probably my hardest loss—by far; I mean it's not much harder than this right now," said Federer, struggling to be coherent. "I'm disappointed," he added. "And I'm crushed."

Nadal, almost apologetic, insisted after it was all over that Federer had been the best player in history and remained the best. "He's still five-time champion here. Right now I have one."

Nadal's graciousness in victory might have made some people wonder whether, in between matches, he took courses in public speaking. He did not. Nadal's post-match generosity toward Federer was the habit, evolved into a reflex, of someone who as a child was ordered by his father to congratulate opponents after a football match when his team had been beaten; it was the consequence of having been taught all his life—by his uncle Toni as by his parents—to keep his feet on the ground, of having had it drummed into him that while his achievements might sometimes be special, he himself was not.

"It was a great moment when we saw him take the Wimbledon trophy in his hands," Sebastián Nadal said, "but when you pause to reflect on it all, it's not that much more special than when they give your child a diploma after graduating from college. Every family has its moments of joy. The day after Rafael won Wimbledon, once all the excitement and the media attention had quieted down, I didn't feel any greater satisfaction than I know I will, for example, the day my daughter gets her university degree. Because, in the end, what you want is for your children to be happy and well."

Nadal's mother, Ana María, also refused to get carried away by her son's achievements. "Sometimes people say to me, 'How lucky you've been with your son!' And I reply, 'I've been lucky with my two children!' I don't give much importance to the fact that Rafael is a super champion, because what makes me happiest in life is the knowledge that I have two children who are good people. They're responsible, they have very close and good friends, they are attached to their family, which is very important for them both, and they haven't given us any problems. This is the real triumph. When all this is over, Rafael will be the same person, my son—and that's it."

The family all flew back to Mallorca the day after the Wimbledon final, and it was straight back to life as usual. Did they have a celebration party? "No," said Sebastián Nadal. "There was the official dinner the night of the match, for which we arrived incredibly late because Rafael had to do so many media interviews, and that was it. We're not very given to celebrations. I remember the match, and always will, but as to what happened afterwards? Nothing much."

Toni Nadal, asked the same question, echoed his elder brother's words. "No, no. I'm not very festive when we win. The satisfaction was enormous, of course. The whole family's. But we Mallorcans, we're not much given to celebration."

Two things did change after Wimbledon, though. Nadal bought himself the sports car he coveted. Despite his misgivings, his father could raise no objections. And Nadal had a new trophy to place alongside the countless others he had won. His godfather, with him sometime later in the sitting room at home where he displays his abundant collection of trophies, asked him which one he valued most. Without a second's hesitation, Nadal pointed to his gold Wimbledon cup and replied, "This one."

CHAPTER 7

MIND OVER MATTER

I F SILENCE IS what defines the Centre Court at Wimbledon, Arthur Ashe Stadium in New York, where I played the final of the US Open in 2010, is defined by noise. Elsewhere, breaks between games are times for quiet pause, but here the show never stops. Hard, pumping music blasts the eardrums, prizes are drawn— with breathless suspense—over the loudspeaker system and Jumbotron. TV screens carry replays of the latest exchanges on court or, to even greater excitement, capture scenes from the crowd: couples kissing, cute kids smiling, celebrities posing, prizewinners celebrating, and, every now and then, New Yorkers fighting. The noise never entirely ceases, fading to a low but constant murmur when the game is on. In theory, as everywhere else in the world, the spectators are asked to remain in their places until play stops and the contestants take their chairs. But Arthur Ashe Stadium is so vast—it's the biggest tennis venue in the world, with a capacity of 23,000—that those sitting in the lower levels are the only ones that pay any heed. Higher up, not only do the fans bustle about at all times, the rule against talking during points seems to exist only to be broken. Not that there would be all that much purpose in enforcing it anyway, given there is no rule against airplanes flying overhead. The tennis complex in Flushing Meadow Park where the US Open is staged is on the flight path to LaGuardia Airport, which means you can be in the middle of a big point, or about to hit a nervous second serve, when the amphitheater is suddenly drowned by the almighty whine of a low-flying jet.

Wimbledon it is not.

The energy, the irreverence, and the relentless din set the US Open apart, as a spectacle, from the other three Grand Slam tournaments. It's pure America—pure New York—and I love it. The noise and the general frenzy test my powers of concentration, certainly, but I'm good at that. By and large, I manage to isolate myself as effectively from my environment at Flushing Meadow as I do at stately Wimbledon. New York is about as far from Manacor as it is possible to imagine, but the presence of my team makes everywhere I go feel a little like home.

The great thing about the professionals who accompany me on the tennis tour is that they make my job feel less like a job, and they give me friendship when the alternative—if they were not so close and loyal, and easy to be with—would be to lead a strangely solitary, nomadic sort of life, jumping from airport to airport, from anonymous hotel room to anonymous hotel room, from players' lounges to restaurants, most of which tend to feel and look exactly the same, wherever in the world I may happen to be.

Jordi Robert, who's always with me in New York, works for Nike, my first ever sponsor, but first and foremost he is a friend. I hope the company values him as much as I do. If a rival to Nike came along and made me a better offer, I'd think long and hard about leaving, simply because of my relationship with Tuts. He's worth gold to them. By virtue of his job description alone, he would not necessarily be expected to be on such intimate terms with me, but he has become an indispensable member of my team. He accompanies me to training, eats at the table with me before and after matches, sits around chatting in my hotel rooms, stays with me in the house we rent at Wimbledon. Tuts is about ten years older than me, but with the stylish glasses he wears and his sassy, brightly colored clothes, you might think I was the older man, for I'm a much more conventional dresser. What I esteem most about Tuts, beyond what he brings to my relationship with Nike, is that he is always smiling, always in a good mood. He is kind and loyal and a comfort to have around. He makes me work, sometimes when—quite honestly—I'd rather be doing something else, but most important of all he is just an incredibly nice guy whose presence helps create the atmosphere of trust and of calm that I need to perform at my best on the tennis court.

Carlos Costa, like Tuts, is not employed directly by me. He works for the big international sports agency, IMG, but he's been by my side since I was fourteen. Carlos negotiates the contracts and makes the first judgments on the requests for sponsorship deals that regularly come our way. But he is also a great friend, and should a problem arise, he is a person I turn to with absolute confidence. His advice is tremendously valuable to me, all the more so because I have learned that the business recommendations he makes are determined not, in the first instance, by the imperative to make money, but by the need to do what's best for my game. It's very hard to find an agent like that. It would be even harder to find one who, like him, has played tennis at the highest level and made it to number ten in the world rankings. As a sporting mentor, he complements Toni very well. He's technically astute and knows the qualities of my rivals. When the tension—the usually valuable tension—that

Toni creates becomes too great, Carlos knows how to defuse it. For example, we'll be in a hotel room in Paris during the French Open and things with Toni suddenly get a bit heated. Carlos will say, "Rafa, let's go for a walk." And the two of us will set off for a stroll around Paris, talk things through, put things in perspective, and I'll return to the hotel in a much better frame of mind. Carlos brings order and stability to our team. Not being family means he is able to make decisions more with his head than with his heart. It would be good to continue in a professional relationship with him beyond my tennis career. Should I set up a business, he is someone I'd want to take with me. Tuts too. Because we'd work well together, but we'd also have a good time.

A big part of the job, in New York as well as anywhere else, is dealing with the media, which is why it's so important for me to have a great professional as my head of communications. Benito Pérez Barbadillo is the most cosmopolitan member of our group. He speaks four languages perfectly, an enormous advantage in a job that requires him to deal with journalists from all over the world, and he has the tough task, which I know he struggles with, of having to play the bad guy for me, turning down journalists constantly, shielding me from the countless requests I get for interviews. If I said yes to them all, I wouldn't have time to do anything else. He understands, as Carlos Costa does, my need to have time not just to train but also to lead a quiet and ordered life on my own, to have the peace necessary to carve out that closed mental space that's essential to my success on the court. When Benito's not around, I miss him. He's irreverent, quick-witted, always cracking jokes. He's informed on what's happening in politics and global affairs generally: in the bubble our team inhabits, he's our connection to the wider world, as he is to the media, and he knows how to administer the news he gives us in just the right measures, and always with a lot of humor and plenty of provocative opinions. But he doesn't take himself too seriously, and we've learned to take much of what he says with a pinch of salt, as he likes to be deliberately outrageous. He's our court jester, the one who lightens the mood in an environment where it's easy to lose perspective and allow things to become too serious and tense.

Francis Roig, my second coach, is a similarly soothing presence, but in a more low-key sort of way. A former pro, like Carlos Costa, he is sharp in his reading of my opponents and an enormously experienced student of the finer points of tennis. He has enormous faith in my abilities and transmits a lot of confidence to me, having added a lot to my understanding of the game. Like Carlos, he is easygoing, a pleasure—as well as an education—to have around ever since we first teamed up on a South American tour in 2005. He is by my side when Toni isn't, which is to say for forty percent or so of the matches on the tour.

Ángel Ruiz Cotorro has been my doctor since I was fourteen years old. He's been by my side during the really tough injuries I've had to endure, providing not just wise medical advice but also the reassurance I've needed to keep fighting, encouraging me to believe in my powers of recovery. He is always available to me, wherever in the world I might be, responding to emergencies large or small. And he has a keen understanding of my particular needs as an athlete, having been the chief medical officer of the Spanish Tennis Federation, dealing regularly with Spain's top players, since before we first met. He is part of the team at many of the top tennis tournaments, but even when he is not around, he is with me in spirit, as is Joan Forcades, my physical trainer, with whom he liaises constantly to assess the condition I am in before conveying long distance instructions to Titín, who is always with me.

Take Titín away from my team and I'd be forlorn. I don't know how his absence would affect my game, but it certainly would my happiness. Always by my side during tournaments, he is the first person I turn to when I have a problem. He's my physical therapist, and he is excellent at what he does, but I value his personal role even more than his professional role, because there are lots of physical therapists in the world, but, were he to move on filling the void of friendship he'd leave behind would be almost impossible. Not only is he a very good person, he is unfailingly honest. If he needs to say something to you, he'll tell it to you straight.

I'd struggle with my tennis if I were one of those players, of whom there are plenty, who is forever changing the members of his team. My principal need for them is at a personal level because tennis is a game in which your emotional state is paramount to success. The better you are within yourself, the better your chances of playing well. I talk a lot about the importance of the word "endurance," but another big word in my vocabulary is "continuity." I simply don't contemplate the notion of changing my team around. I've always had, and hope always to have, the same team around me. Toni, who's been with me forever, established the pattern, and I don't ever want to see it broken.

We have a pattern when we're in New York for the US Open too. We always stay in hotels within the same mid-Manhattan neighborhoods, near Central Park, and after driving to and from Flushing Meadow during the day, we go in the evening to one of the four or five restaurants that we always go to, within walking distance of the hotel, usually to eat Japanese food, because there is nothing better than the quality of fish you'll get at a good Japanese restaurant. The rest of the time we'll hang around a lot in my hotel room, chatting or watching movies or a football game. We also watch plenty of videos of matches I've played in, with Toni and me watching closely, drawing lessons from my mistakes but also from my better moments of play. It's good for morale to watch myself playing a great point or strike a winning forehand drive, but more important, it helps me visualize the finer aspects of my game, allowing me to record a mental picture in my head that I then use when I go out on court, in order to recapture that fluent feeling of control I need to strike the ball well. It's hard to explain, but it works.

When I am in Manhattan, I'd love to be able to walk around more and absorb the energy of the place, see the sights, but people don't tend to hold back when they catch sight of sports stars, and trying to behave like a normal person and pass by unperceived on a stroll down Fifth Avenue is, as I know from experience, mission impossible. It's no use complaining about this, any more than there's any point in getting irritated when rain stops play. It goes with the job and you accept it. That means the only times I might wander far from the vicinity of my hotel will be when one of my sponsors asks me to take part in some promotional event they might be staging in a downtown warehouse or, as in the case of an extravaganza Nike organized, on the wharf on the Hudson River where the *Titanic* would have docked had it completed its maiden voyage. Again, everyone will come along. Not just Tuts, but Titín, Carlos, Benito, and whoever else might be around. Whatever we do, we're all in it together.

This year, the 2010 US Open was incredibly hot the first week, but then it cooled down and, on the day of the final, it rained so much that the match had to be postponed by twenty-four hours. This

Roland Garros 2005:
my first Grand Slam.

My first French
Open trophy, 2005.

On my way to
the Wimbledon
final, 2008.

Moments of triumph at the Wimbledon 2008 final.

Shaking hands with Federer at the end of the Wimbledon final, 2008.

With the Spanish flag after embracing my family at Wimbledon's Centre Court, 2008. Also in the picture: my father, my mother, Toni, Tuts, and Titín, just visible.

The Australian Open final vs. Federer in 2009, playing through the exhaustion.

Australia 2009: I collect my third Grand Slam.

On my way to a comfortable French Open final victory against Robin Soderling in 2010, my best year.

I commiserate with Federer after the Australian Open final, 2009.

Winning the French
Open final 2010, the
first of three Grand
Slams that year.

Relaxed after
winning the
French Open,
2010.

Another
Grand Slam
final victory,
against Tomas
Berdych at
Wimbledon,
2010.

I win my
second
Wimbledon,
2010.

Celebrating
Wimbledon
victory, 2010.

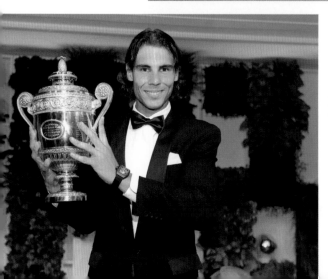

Holding the
Wimbledon trophy
at the gala dinner
on the night of the
final.

I celebrate winning the US Open, 2010, against Novak Djokovic in four sets.

On my knees at Arthur Ashe Stadium, Flushing Meadows, New York, 2010.

I bite the US Open trophy, the one that completes my Grand Slam.

was not a bad thing for my opponent, Novak Djokovic, who had had a much longer, tougher semifinal than I'd had, beating Roger Federer in five sets. In his place, I'd have welcomed the extra day's rest.

A strong and fit Djokovic was a formidable opponent. Our match didn't have quite the same aura as another Federer-Nadal battle, at least as far as the crowds were concerned, but for me the challenge was quite daunting enough. He is a very complete player—more complete, Toni says, than I am—without any obvious weak points, and on hard surfaces, such as the ones at Flushing Meadow, he'd beaten me more times than I had beaten him. His greatest strengths are his excellent sense of positioning on the court and his ability to hit the ball early, on the rise. He is as good on the backhand as on the forehand, and his vision of the ball is so sharp that he plays with time to spare, more often than not inside the court, narrowing the angles for his opponents, making the game a lot easier for himself.

With Federer, the rule is always to keep patiently plugging away, knowing you'll force him sooner or later to make mistakes. With Djokovic, there is no clear tactical plan. It is simply a question of playing at your very best, with maximum intensity and aggression, seeking to retain control of the point, because the moment you let him get the upper hand, he is unstoppable.

My impressions were confirmed as I watched his semifinal against Federer on TV, which Djokovic won after saving two match points. I thought, not for the first time, "What an incredibly tough and talented guy!" I also thought how hard it was going to be to beat him. When I watch the top players on video, I often have the feeling that they're better than me. It was not a very logical thing to be thinking during the US Open, given that I was world number one by now and had been for most of the previous two years. I'd also beaten both of them more times than they had beaten me. Neither am I at all sure this is the way most champion athletes regard their rivals. I expect it's the other way around. In my case it's probably got a lot to do with Toni, who's conditioned me to believe from childhood that every match is going to be an uphill battle. I am not sure this is always the healthiest frame of mind in which to enter a match, because sometimes it puts a check on my confidence, leading me to play with less aggression than I might. But, on the plus side, it means that I treat everyone I play with respect and never succumb to complacency. It may be the reason why I rarely lose against players who, by their position in the rankings, I should beat.

Yet I wasn't especially nervous—not in the light of the challenge that lay ahead of me, at any rate—before the 2010 final against Djokovic. I was certainly a lot less wound up than before the 2008 Wimbledon final. I slept well, a good eight hours, on both nights before. There were two because of the day's rain delay. Each time I put on a movie in my hotel room and, instead of tossing and turning and imagining the worst, went straight to sleep. Partly it was that my mind wasn't haunted, as it had been at Wimbledon, by the memory of past traumas. Partly it was my greater experience and maturity, the number of Grand Slam finals I'd played in; but partly too it was that my expectations were not so high. Images of winning Wimbledon had played in my mind since my teens; the US Open had always felt like a dream too far.

This is not to say that I went into the match against Djokovic in a defeatist frame of mind. Obviously I felt I could win, but I had the sense that if I did, it would be a happy and unexpected plus in my career, rather than something I had to achieve or live the rest of my life ridden by a sense of failure.

I'd always regarded the US Open as the most difficult tournament for me to win. At Wimbledon I'd played very well even when
I hadn't won; at the US Open I had never really played my best.
Twice before I'd made it to the semifinals, but in neither case did I
feel entirely comfortable on court. It has to do with the exceptionally fast surface but also with the balls they use at the US Open,
which are softer than the ones used elsewhere, preventing me from
applying as much heavy topspin, and therefore as much height, to
my shots as I usually do. That's the aspect of my game that gives my
opponents the most trouble, and where I have an edge over most of
them. There's another factor too: the US Open is the last of the four
Grand Slams, coming toward the end of the long, hard summer
season, and I tend to arrive in New York tired, both physically and
mentally.

I had arrived more than usually wiped out for the 2008 tournament, in which I lost in the semifinals to Andy Murray, and not just
because of the nervous energy I'd invested in winning Wimbledon.
In between the two competitions I'd traveled halfway around the
world to play in the Beijing Olympic Games, my first experience of
taking part in the biggest sports show on earth. I enjoyed it immensely and it taught me a lot—most of all, how lucky I am.

I stayed in the Olympic village with all the other athletes, and
once again, as in the Davis Cup, I had a taste of that team spirit
that I loved so much when I played football as a kid. Living with
my Spanish teammates, in the same residential compound, meeting and making friends with the Spanish basketball team and
track athletes (some of whom, a little embarrassingly, would stop
me in the corridors, or in the communal laundry room where we
all washed our clothes, to ask me for my autograph) and stepping out
in uniform alongside them all for the opening ceremony—these

were unforgettable experiences. But my sense of good fortune came accompanied by a strong dose of indignation.

I understood better than ever just how privileged we professional tennis players are, and how unjust is the predicament of so many Olympic athletes. They train incredibly hard, at least as hard as we do, yet the rewards tend to be far smaller. A tennis player ranked number eighty in the world has economic benefits, social privileges, and a degree of recognition beyond the dreams of someone who is number one in track and field, swimming, or gymnastics. On the tennis circuit everything is laid on for us all year round, and the money we receive allows us the chance to save for our futures. These people train with the discipline of monks over a period of four years in preparation for the one competition that stands out above all others, the Olympics, yet the vast majority of them receive very little support relative to the effort they invest. It's admirable that they should prepare so rigorously, at so much personal sacrifice, for the mere satisfaction of competing and because of the passion they feel for their sports. That has a value beyond price. But that shouldn't have to be enough. With all the income the International Olympic Committee generates from the Games—an event that depends for its success on the commitment of the athletes—you'd think they might be able to share the cash a little more fairly. In my case, I have no need to be paid, luckily, but an athlete who runs in the 400 meters or the marathon needs a lot of financial backing just to be able to train at the level required to make it to the Olympics and then compete for the top prizes. I understand that tennis has broader public appeal, at least over the course of a calendar year, but I think it's unjust that more of an effort is not made to allow these incredibly dedicated people to live more decently and train in better conditions.

But these were my reflections after it was all over. Moaning and griping was not what defined my time in Beijing. What stays with me, above all, was the camaraderie between the athletes and the chance I had to learn about so many different new sports and discover how much we all had in common. Just to be able to participate, and to have access to a world I never thought I'd get to know, was uplifting enough. Then to win gold in the men's singles, after beating Djokovic in the semis and Fernando Gonzalez of Chile in the final, and to see the Spanish flag being raised to the accompaniment of the national anthem as I stood on the winner's podium: well, it was one of my life's proudest moments. People don't usually associate the Olympic Games with tennis. I certainly didn't when I was growing up. The game only reappeared as an Olympic sport in 1988, after a sixty-four-year absence. But in tennis players' minds Olympic gold has become something to covet. After a Grand Slam, it's now the prize we most cherish.

The first Grand Slam of the year is the Australian Open, held in Melbourne. It's a nice tournament, less raucous than the US Open, more easygoing than Wimbledon, less grand than Paris—though they put me up in a hotel suite so huge I could almost play a game of five-a-side football in it. I enjoy the food in Melbourne. There's another great Japanese place downstairs from the hotel. I also appreciate the quick, five-minute drive through lush green parkland to Melbourne Park, the club where the competition is held. And it's hot, coming straight from the European winter. I usually arrive a week before the tournament begins in order to adapt to the ten-hour time difference with Spain. The effort to adjust is complicated, in my case, by the fact that January is an important month in the football calendar back home, and I find myself having to get up at odd hours of the morning to watch Real Madrid play. If they are playing very early, what I'll do is set the alarm clock, see how the match is going, and decide then whether to stay up or remain in bed. If they're winning 3–0 with half an hour to go, I'll turn over and go back to sleep. If it's 0–0, the suspense will be too much for me and I'll have to stay up to watch to the end. But I won't get up outrageously early, however big the football game might be, if I'm competing myself that day. The job comes first.

Going into the Australian Open in 2009, I felt my chances of winning were as good as they had been at Wimbledon six months earlier. I had, in other words, a good fighting chance. The surface of the courts was hard, but less complicated for my game than Flushing Meadow. The ball bounces higher than it does at the US Open, so it doesn't fly so fast and it takes my topspin well. What I hadn't reckoned on was a semifinal like the one I had against my friend and fellow Spaniard Fernando Verdasco. I won, in the end, but I had to battle so hard and was left so physically destroyed by the end of it. For most of the one and a half days of preparation I had for the final against Federer, I was convinced I had absolutely no chance of winning. The only time I'd felt like that before a Grand Slam final was at Wimbledon in 2006, but that was because I did not believe, in my heart of hearts, that winning was an option. Before the Australian final in 2009 it was my body that rebelled, begging me to call a halt. It didn't cross my mind to pull out of the match—short of imminent collapse, you can't do that in a Grand Slam final—but the result I anticipated, and for which I strove mentally to prepare myself, was a 6–1, 6–2, 6–2 defeat.

The semifinal I played against Verdasco was the longest match in Australian Open history. It was incredibly tight every step of the way, with him playing spectacularly, hitting an extraordinarily high percentage of outright winners. But I somehow held on, on the defense but making few errors, and after five hours and fourteen minutes, I won 6–7, 6–4, 7–6, 6–7, 6–4. It was so hot on court that the two of us rushed to drape ice packs around our necks and shoulders in the breaks between games. In the very last game, just before the very last point, my eyes filled with tears. I wasn't crying because I sensed defeat, or even victory, but as a response to the sheer excruciating tension of it all. I had lost the fourth set on a tie break, and that, in a game so tense and in such conditions, would have been devastating had I not been able to call on every last reserve of mental strength I'd accumulated over fifteen years of relentless competition. I was able to put that blow behind me and begin the fifth believing I still had it in me to win.

The chance finally arrived with me 5–4 and 0–40 up on Verdasco's serve. That should have been it, with three match points, but it wasn't quite. I lost both the first and the second points. That was when it all got too much for me and I broke down; that was where the armor plating fell away and the warrior Rafa Nadal, who tennis fans think they know, lay revealed as the vulnerable, human Rafael. The one person who didn't see it was Verdasco. Either that or he was in even worse shape than I was. Because his nerves got the better of him too. In a moment of incredible good luck for me (and terrible luck for him), he double faulted, handing me victory without me having to hit a shot. Both of us fell flat on our backs, ready to expire of physical and nervous exhaustion, but it was me who made it up first, stumbling forward and stepping over the net to embrace Fernando and tell him it was a match neither of us had deserved to lose. Toni, who had not failed to notice the quivering wreck I'd been reduced to in the final game, remarked later that had Verdasco not double faulted, the semifinal would probably have been his. I tend to agree.

The match ended at one in the morning, and I did not go to sleep till after five. First I had to do the obligatory post-match press conference, plus interviews with individual journalists. My legs could hardly carry me, and God knows what I said. Back, at last, in my hotel room, I had some food brought up. Sleep would have to wait. I ate, replenishing my empty batteries, and then I abandoned myself to Titín, whose task it was to bring my battered body back to life and start preparing me for the match against Federer. Tuts saw me in the locker room after the Verdasco match, dead to the world, and his first thought was "My God! Titín's got the job of his life here!" Tuts was right.

Fortunately, Titín was calm and collected as usual. He did what he always does in difficult circumstances, he enlisted the help of Joan Forcades, my physical trainer, whom he reached in Mallorca with a Skype call from his computer. Forcades and Titín are friends and allies, their shared mission to attend to the needs of my body, to prevent injuries, maximize my fitness levels, and help me recover in time for my next match when my body's taken a beating. Right now I was more exhausted than I had ever been at any point in my life. The challenge they faced—the three of us faced—required, it seemed to me, a miracle. But Joan was not downhearted.

Joan has known me since I was nine or ten years old, and he has more faith in me than I have in myself. He is fantastic at his job and is a very, very important member of my team, but he operates more in the shadows than the rest. He used to travel with me, but now he does so very rarely, preferring to stay at home in Mallorca, away from the fame and far from the media. He's a special guy who has a day job that he loves—as a schoolteacher in a public school in Mallorca—and he doesn't work with me for the money but because he enjoys it and cares for me as if I were family.

I overheard his conversation with Titín. Lots of ice was what was needed, they agreed, and lots of massage, to get the blood pumping through the system again. Joan, who had been analyzing the situation with Dr. Cotorro, was adamant that I'd have to take a good dose of protein and vitamin supplements, but most of all, he said, the important thing was to get the body moving again. He recommended that next day we do some stretching exercises to stir the muscles back into life, then some pedaling on the exercise bicycle, followed by a practice session on court. Joan was optimistic, reminding Titín that in our pre-season training over the Christmas period we had been preparing for this, training hard in the morning for three or four hours, then again in the afternoons for an hour and a half. "The most important thing is that we get his body in action again," Joan said.

I heard that, and I saw his logic, but at the time, three in the morning Australian time, all I was in any fit state for was submitting passively, immobile on a couch, to Titín's therapeutic skills. The first thing he did after hanging up with Joan was to fill the bathtub with ice and make me sit in it, as a first step to activate the blood flow in my aching thighs. Then massages, first with a bag of ice, then using a bar of soap. Usually the day before a final I'll train in the morning. This time I slept all morning, waking up in the early afternoon to discover, aghast, that I felt stiffer than the night before. Still, I pedaled away at the bike, smoothly, Titín said, just to get the blood circulating, and then I went out on court, with Carlos Costa on the other side of the net. I lasted barely twenty minutes. It was Carlos who saw I couldn't go on. "It's no good. You can't move," he said. "We've got to stop." Dizzy, utterly drained, my calves feeling like lead, I hobbled off court and drove back to the hotel and straight into the ice bath. Titín was working overtime to get me ready for the next day's final, but at that moment, crushed by my breakdown on court, I felt as if there could be no force on earth or heaven capable of accomplishing the task.

I went to sleep that night in the grimmest of moods and woke up the next morning feeling only marginally less stiff. When I went out on the practice court for my last training session at five in the afternoon, two and a half hours before the match was due to start, I hardly felt any better. Again, I felt dizzy; again, my leg muscles felt heavy and hard—so much so that I suddenly had an attack of cramps in one of my calves. Toni was there, and after half an hour struggling to get some rhythm going, I told him I couldn't go on. I must have looked terrible because he said, "OK. Stop. Let's go back to the locker room." And there it was that Toni rose to the occasion.

My uncle's power has always come from the word, from what he says to motivate me. He tells me these days that the most valuable training we did when I was a kid was not on the court but during the sessions we had in the car going to and from games on the fifty-kilometer drive to Palma, planning beforehand what we would do or analyzing afterward what we had done wrong. I remember he used examples from football, from Real Madrid, to catch my attention and ram home his thoughts. And Toni is right. His words taught me to think for myself on court and they taught me to be a fighter. He likes to quote some Spanish writer who said that the people who start wars are always poets. Well, poetry, of sorts, was what he used on me now, at this seemingly hopeless moment when battle had not even been engaged but, in my mind, I had already lost.

"Look," he said, "it's five thirty now, and when you go on court at seven thirty I assure you you won't be feeling any better. You'll probably be feeling worse. So it's up to you whether you rise above the pain and the exhaustion and summon up the desire you need to win." I replied, "Toni, I'm sorry. I can't see it. I just can't." "Don't say you can't," he said. "Because anybody who digs deep enough can always find the motivation they need for anything. In war, people do things that appear to be impossible. Just imagine if there were a guy sitting behind you in the stadium pointing a gun at you, telling you that if you didn't run, and keep running, he'd shoot you. I bet you'd run then. So, come on! It's up to you to find the motivation to win. This is your big chance. Bad as you might be feeling now, it's likely that you'll never have as good a chance of winning the Australian Open as you do today. And even if there's only a one percent chance of you winning this match, well, then, you have to squeeze every last drop out of that one percent." Toni saw me hesitate, saw me listening, so he pressed on. "Remember that phrase of Barack Obama's, 'Yes, we can!' At every changeover repeat it to yourself, because, you know what? The truth is you *can* do it. What you can never allow is to fail because of a loss of will. You can lose because your rival played better, but you can't lose because you failed to give it your best. That would be a crime. But you won't do that, I know it. Because you always do give your best and today will be no exception. You can, Rafael! You really can!"

I was listening. It was as stirring a speech as Toni had ever given me. Whether my body was paying much attention was another matter. That was where Joan Forcades came in again. Titín remained in constant communication with him via Skype. Joan, who has a habit of peppering his conversation with complicated scientific jargon, stressed the need to play the match "ergonomically," by which he meant I needed to adjust my game to the realities of the physical condition I was in. This meant pacing myself more than I usually would, saving my body's reserves of energy for the more critical points, not fighting for every single point as if it were my last. And also trying to make the points shorter, which meant taking more risks.

Armed with a plan, I took my usual cold shower, after which I did feel better, and performed my sequence of pre-match rituals in the locker room with a sense of growing conviction. And when I went out on court, I wasn't hobbling anymore. The aches were still there and I felt a little sluggish during the warm-up with Federer. Sure enough, my left foot—that tarsal scaphoid bone—began bothering me again. But I'd been here before, and I hoped that the adrenaline and my powers of concentration would triumph over the pain one more time. I still wondered whether my body would hold up, but the good news was that, overall, I was feeling sharper than I had two hours earlier and a lot more so than when I had woken up after sleeping all morning the day before. Most important of all, the defeatism I'd felt earlier on had gone. I'd recovered the will to win and the belief that I could do so. Suddenly the challenge of overcoming the predicament I was in became something not to fear, but to relish. Toni's words, Titín's work, and Joan's advice had done their magic.

No sooner had the match got under way than the aches began to recede. So much so that I won the first game, breaking Federer's serve. Then he broke me back, but as the games unfolded I found, to my great relief, that I wasn't panting and out of breath, and while my calves still felt heavy, there were no signs of the muscle cramps I had feared. And none materialized, despite the match going to five sets. In the end, as Titín says, pain is in the mind. If you can control the mind, you can control the body. I lost the fourth set, as I had done against Verdasco, after going two sets to one up, but I came back, my determination bolstered and my spirit enhanced by the surprise and delight I felt at having made it as far as I had without falling apart. At 2–0 up in the fifth set I turned to where Toni, Carlos, Tuts, and Titín were sitting and said, just loud enough so they could hear, in Mallorquín, "I'm going to win." And I did. Toni had been right. Yes, I could. I won 7–5, 3–6, 7–6, 3–6, 6–2, and I was Australian Open champion; to my astonishment I had come back to life, and there it was, my third of the four Grand Slam titles, now my sixth in all.

Roger Federer was as mentally broken after the match was over as I had been physically before it. I'd have felt the same way in his place. He'd played a bad final set, and by beating him I had consolidated my standing as world number one. Yet those who started writing him off after that defeat, and there were a few, proved to be wrong. He had plenty of fire left in him. This had been his chance to match Pete Sampras's record of fourteen Grand Slams and he'd failed, at least for now. To me, he was still the best of all time, as I reminded people when my time came to be interviewed, and he showed it to the world over the next couple of years, adding more major trophies to his cabinet and beating Sampras's record.

As for me, I took a big lesson from that victory. It was a lesson Toni had been drumming into me for years, but never had I discovered how true it was until now. I learned that you always have to hang in there, that however remote your chances of winning might seem, you have to push yourself to the very limit of your abilities and try your luck. That day in Melbourne I saw, more clearly than ever before, that the key to this game resides in the mind, and if the mind is clear and strong, you can overcome almost any obstacle, including pain. Mind can triumph over matter.

A year and a half later, before the final of the 2010 US Open, it seemed not to be me but my rival Novak Djokovic who'd have to overcome the pain barrier. He was in the position I had been in approaching the Australian Open final. In Flushing Meadow, I was the one who was relatively fresh, having made it to the final without dropping a set, whereas Djokovic was coming straight from that five-set semifinal against Federer, in which he had saved two match points before winning. But he was luckier than I had been in Melbourne. The day's delay because of the rain in New York was a blessing for him, and by the time we got out on court on Monday, September 13, we were on equal terms physically.

The atmosphere was not as tense among my team as it had been before the Wimbledon final of 2008. My parents were there, and so were my sister Maribel and my girlfriend María Francisca this time, and in between training and competing at Flushing Meadow, we ventured out once or twice—braving the mobs—to the shops on Fifth Avenue, as well as to our favorite restaurants, and we even caught a Broadway show. (We might have stayed in a hotel in Flushing Meadow, avoiding the traffic on the drive to the tennis center, but to compete in the US Open and not stay in Manhattan was to miss out on too much fun.) Again unlike the experience in Wimbledon, not only did I sleep well before the final with Djokovic, as I had done throughout the two weeks of the tournament, but I was also able to talk quite openly about the match. There was no taboo about it as there had been at Wimbledon. I wasn't dogged by memories of collapsing in the shower and weeping. But there was one thing we didn't talk about. I didn't have to issue any prohibitions, but everybody understood instinctively that the one thing we wouldn't mention was the one thing on everybody's mind, including my own: that if I defeated Djokovic I'd complete what in America they call the Golden Slam; I'd become the seventh player ever to win all four major tennis titles and, at twenty-four, the youngest ever to achieve it since the start of "the

Open Era" in 1968, the year professionals were first allowed to compete in Grand Slam tournaments. In this period only Rod Laver, Andre Agassi, and Roger Federer had managed to win all four. Winning the US Open, the most difficult of the big tournaments for me, would be a remarkable enough thing, but doing so after I'd won Wimbledon, Paris, and Australia, would be—it was perfectly clear to all of us—the crowning achievement of my career.

Yet no one mentioned the subject in my company, and the rest of them, as they told me later, never even talked about it among themselves. In a measure of how united we all are, to what degree every member of my family and my team really is a part of me, each had reached his or her own conclusion that they all should keep their thoughts to themselves. They sensed that by airing them they would put the entire enterprise at risk. We'll never know whether our conspiracy of silence was justified, or even necessary, but what everyone around me understands is that before a match of this magnitude my mental state is as taut as it is fragile and they must treat me with extreme delicacy and care. That's why Toni, Titín, Carlos, Benito, and Tuts must be friends as well as professionals, why I need a team around me sensitive to my way of being as well as diligent in their attention to my needs, why I want my family close by. That is also why I have to follow my locker room rituals in the same order always, why I must sip from each of my two bottles of water in each and every break between games. It's like a great big matchstick structure: if every piece is not symmetrically in place, it can all fall down.

MURDER ON THE ORIENT EXPRESS

THE ICE BATHS, the massaging of the leaden legs, the vitamin supplements, and the pedaling on the exercise bicycle all played their part in achieving the miracle of Melbourne. But Joan Forcades, rather than take credit for the advice he dispensed in the moment of crisis, views the physical dimension of Rafa Nadal's recovery and triumph in the Australian Open as just one element in a complex picture. "You've got to think *Murder on the Orient Express*," Nadal's physical trainer says, "to understand the secret of Rafael's success."

Forcades is neither pretentious nor deliberately cryptic. In fact, his reference to the Agatha Christie murder mystery is an unusually illuminating departure for a man who peppers his conversation quite naturally with terms like "holistic," "cognitive," "somatic marker," "asymmetric," and "emotive-volitive." His brain is forever finding connections between the world of elite sports and Shakespearean tragedy, or German philosophy, or Thomas Aquinas, or the latest trends in neurobiological research.

"The point about *Murder on the Orient Express* is that there was one man murdered, but Hercule Poirot, the detective, discovered

that a dozen people took part in the crime—all the suspects killed
him," says Forcades, who explains: "That's the approach you have
to take to get to the bottom of Rafael's victory in Australia, and all
the other victories he has had in his career. If you focus only one
aspect, on how he recuperated physically, you're missing a much
bigger story."

Forcades spends long hours with Nadal when he is back home in
Mallorca, but is otherwise removed from the bustle and drama of
the international tennis tour. His distance and his analytical frame
of mind single him out as the member of Nadal's inner circle best
placed to play the part of Hercule Poirot and uncover the secret
of the success of the young man he has spent more than a decade
training. In sifting through the evidence and putting the pieces of
the puzzle together, he is guided by a core thought: the Nadal phenomenon is greater than the sum of its parts. This is where the
fascination lies for Forcades—not in the details of Nadal's training
regimen. It bores him—to the point of irritation—to explain why
Nadal doesn't lift weights, or why he doesn't run, save in very short
bursts, or why he does exercise X or exercise Y to strengthen his
ankles or his tendons, or why he uses particular machines or vi-
brating platforms or elastic chords to develop his muscular strength
so that he can play for five hours at full tilt or maximize the speed
of acceleration of his left arm. What is more interesting to Forcades
is the manic intensity Nadal brings to his work in the gymnasium,
on good days and bad, and how he sustains that intensity with cold
clarity of purpose, transforming it into triumph on the tennis court.
And, most interesting of all, is the question, where does it all come
from? Yes, he is a great tennis player because he has great tennis
genes, but that alone does not explain why he is a serial winner of
Grand Slams. There are plenty of people born with the talent to

play tennis at the highest level, and some of the rivals he routinely beats have more natural talent, arguably.

"This question of who exploits his talent and who does not is like the making of popcorn," says Forcades. "Some kernels burst, some don't. Why has Rafa's kernel exploded so spectacularly?"

The first place to look for the answers is not in the legs or the arms but the head, "the most fragile part of the body," in Forcades's words, and the most decisive in determining victory or defeat in elite sports, especially in an individual sport like tennis.

"Tennis is all about resolving emergencies, one emergency after another over a prolonged period of time. No point is ever the same, and decisions have to be taken constantly in fractions of seconds. The player who, when he makes a mistake, is capable of not remaining anchored in the recollection of the mistake, or who, when he strikes a great shot and gets ahead in a set, is able to control the rush of optimism and is able to continue playing steadily, judging each shot independently in the moment, at speed and under brutal time pressure: that is the player who is going to stand out above the rest and be a champion not once, not twice, but over time. In this decision-making frenzy, having a cool head is vital, and having a cool head depends on your emotional well-being. This is the single most important attribute that Rafael possesses. His state of alertness, sustained for hours at a time, is almost superhuman. It is the key to everything."

If Nadal has triumphed, it is because his head, his body, and his emotions, indivisibly interconnected, have been in tune or, as Forcades puts it, "in perfect synergy." And the reason for this has been the consistently favorable influence of a happy childhood and ordered adolescence, and his enduring relationship with each member of his family and his team. This is what Forcades calls the "socio-affective" factor, which means, translated, that, unusual among elite athletes, Rafa has lived all his life within the shelter of a remarkably stable, remarkably conflict-free environment. "And one in which his parents and his uncle Toni conveyed the message from very early on that talent, without humility and hard work, will never flower. Humility is the recognition of your limitations, and it is from this understanding, and this understanding alone, that the drive comes to work hard at overcoming them. That is why Rafael—a role model for children everywhere—works with more passionate commitment in the gym than any tennis player I have ever come across; why, for all the success he has had, he strives with the utmost seriousness in every single practice session to make improvements to his game."

That "continuity" Nadal values so much in his life is something almost unknown among elite athletes, Forcades says. His coach, twenty years with him; his physical trainer and his agent, ten; his physical therapist and his press chief, five; and his family united behind him, almost a part of him, with no squabbles or jealousies in view from the day he was born. "Success of the type Rafael has, success that you know is going to put you in the history books: that's very hard to handle. It feeds the ego and can drive you mad. That's where you need the stability of a family who keep your feet on the ground. That is where Rafael has been particularly fortunate to have an uncle close to him who has tasted success and money and fame in the football world. People sometimes wonder whether champions are born or are made. Miguel Ángel's example taught him early on you can't make the distinction; that both things are true. Because if you are born with certain talents but you don't train and be passionate about what you do, you won't get anywhere. A great thing about Rafael is that the desire to keep learning and keep improving is something that's in his blood. He knows that no one is a god, much less he himself, but his spirit of self-sacrifice—I've seen it myself, year after year, however high he might have scaled the Olympus—is superhuman."

Uncle Miguel Ángel, uncle Toni, the grounded mother and father, the wider support group of the extended family, the steady girlfriend, the fixed professional team who are all friends. and also, as Forcades remarks, the coy, self-effacing nature of the Mallorcan, combined with Nadal's native talent and intelligence and drive, all add up to a sum much greater than the visible parts. "Rafael's intricate emotional safety net has freed his mind and body to allow him to get the best out of himself. Without it, the effectiveness of my physical training with him would be a fraction of what it is. Without it, it is unimaginable that he would have developed into the uniquely fit and strong tennis player that he is, capable of the mental sharpness necessary to make the snap decisions that determine the outcome, under circumstances of heavy expectation and extreme nerves, in the final of a Grand Slam tennis tournament. Because, the point is, you cannot separate the person from the athlete. And the person comes first. Rafa has succeeded because he is a good person, with a good family behind him."

CHAPTER 8

PARADISE LOST

THE MUSIC CEASED, a sure sign that the match at Arthur Ashe Stadium was about to begin. My eardrums had received a pounding during the warm-up—no hearing the echo of your own shot here—but now we were off. The 2010 US Open final had begun, with Djokovic serving. And in bright afternoon sunshine, after the previous day's rain.

The first point, stretching to twenty-one shots, was a great one for the fans but not so much for me, since Djokovic won it, but I always try to see things in the best light, and there had been much to salvage. I had gone through practically my whole repertory of shots during the rally, starting with a deep and low sliced backhand return of his first serve, some solid forehands, a powerfully punched backhand. I'd struck them all well and I'd controlled the point, keeping him on the defensive—until I went for a drop. Not a hesitant or a craven drop; a calculated, attacking one. But he was too quick— Djokovic is very quick, it was just as well to be reminded of this early on—and I was able only to snatch lamely at his lobbed return high on the backhand, allowing him to put away a simple mid-court winner.

Fifteen-love down but no reason at all to feel discouraged. I was feeling those good sensations again, seeing and hearing the ball well. To "hear" the ball, a term Joan Forcades likes, is to strike just the right note in each shot you make; it means the contact between racket and ball is fluent, that your head and body are in tune.

I wasn't deceiving myself about the odds. Djokovic went for too much on the next point and hit a forehand long; then he himself tried a drop shot, a poor one that let me whip a cross-court backhand way past his reach, then a wild and long backhand followed by my winner down. I'd broken him on the first game, and a better start would have been impossible. Now at 1–0 up, it was my serve: another cause to celebrate, for rarely in my career had I served better than at this US Open. On my way to the final I had not dropped a set and had only lost my serve twice in ninety-one games. There was a reason for this.

I had taken a decision at the start of the tournament to make a slight alteration to my grip, trading a measure of slice for greater power, getting the head of the racket to strike the ball more full-on. It was risky, but it worked. My service has never been one of my strong points. It is not a shot I deliver with as much conviction as my ground stroke. My movements are not as mechanized as Federer's, for example, and sometimes, especially when things get tense, I can lose my rhythm. I don't toss the ball as high as I should and my body tightens up. This might be an instance where playing tennis left-handed, while being right-handed in most other things, confuses the mental circuitry. Something doesn't always work as reliably as it might in the coordination between brain and body.

But in this US Open I served like a dream, blasting down lots of good first serves and winning a lot more "free points" than I usually do. The economy of the big serve was something I had long

envied in other players, but not during this tournament. The up-
shot was that I covered less ground than I usually do on my way to
a final, allowing me to conserve energy and arrive at the match
against Djokovic in a state of physical well-being that could not
have been further removed from the way I had felt going into the
Australian Open final the year before.

Never had I embarked on a US Open campaign feeling fresher.
My body and mind were relaxed, and when I arrived in New York
on the Monday a week before the tournament began, I played a
round of golf, and another one the next day. Then, Toni's arrival
from Mallorca on the Wednesday signaled a return to maximum
intensity and full-on, peak training.

The particular work I had put into my serve paid off in the second
game of the final. I seized the early chance Djokovic had unexpectedly handed me to go 2–0 up. But then he came back, winning his
serve and breaking my next one, after playing some blinding shots,
to put the score at 2–2. Amazingly for a match of this importance on
a surface that suits the server, I then broke him again—three breaks
in five games. I won it with a deep winner to his forehand side after
a brutally long game, with one deuce after another. Order was re-
stored, all the games went to the server, and I won the set 6–4.

The record showed that I'd only lost one Grand Slam match out
of 107 after winning the first set. But it was not wise to dwell on
that statistic. There was always a first—or, in this case, second—time
for everything. Djokovic was not only a supremely talented player
capable of the most dazzling tennis on his day, but he'd also beaten
me convincingly in our last three encounters on hard surfaces. I was
grateful to have my chance to redress the balance; grateful, in the
light of not too distant calamities, to be here at all. To have imagined I'd be in this final, going for the foursome of Grand Slams,

would have been a stretch twelve months earlier, midway through 2009, a year that started fabulously, with the Australian Open victory, and then went from bad to worse.

On the first leg of the long journey back from Australia, on the flight from Melbourne to Dubai, my father told me there were problems back home between himself and my mother. I quickly figured out he meant a separation was in the cards. Fortunately he had the tact not to tell me a couple of days earlier, before the final; otherwise, I would not have found the strength to recover from the semifinal with Verdasco. But that was only the tiniest of consolations. The news left me stunned. I didn't talk to my father on the rest of the trip home.

My parents were the pillar of my life and that pillar had crumbled. The continuity I so valued in my life had been cut in half, and the emotional order I depend on had been dealt a shocking blow. Another family with grown-up children (I was twenty-two and my sister, eighteen) might have taken a marital separation more in its stride. But this was not possible in a family as close and united as ours, where there had been no conflict visible, where all we had ever seen was harmony and good cheer. Assimilating the news that my parents had been going through such a crisis after nearly thirty years of marriage was heartbreaking. My family had always been the holy, untouchable core of my life, my center of stability and a living album of my wonderful childhood memories. Suddenly, and utterly without warning, the happy family portrait had cracked. I suffered on behalf of my father, my mother, and my sister, who were all having a terrible time. But everybody was affected: my uncles and aunt, my grandparents, my nephews and nieces. Our whole world was destabilized, and contact between members of the family became, for the first time that I had been aware of, awkward and unnatural; no one knew at first how to react. Returning back home had always been a joy; now it became uncomfortable and strange.

Through all these years of constant travel and ever more frenzied claims on my time as my fame had grown, Manacor and our neighboring seaside resort of Porto Cristo was a bubble of peace and sanity, a private world where I could isolate myself from the celebrity madness and be entirely myself again. Fishing, golf, friends, the old routine of family lunches and dinners—all that had changed. My father had moved out of our Porto Cristo home, and now when we sat down to eat or watch TV, he wasn't there. Where there had been laughter and jokes, a heavy silence hung. Paradise had become paradise lost.

Strangely, the effect on my game was not immediate. I was on a winning streak, and the positive momentum carried me through for a couple of months. I won in Monte Carlo, Barcelona, and Rome, and more surprisingly, I won on the hard surface of Indian Wells. I felt no elation at the moment of victory, but my body somehow kept going through the motions. My attitude was bad. I was depressed, lacking in enthusiasm. On the surface I remained a tennis-playing automaton, but the man inside had lost all love of life.

My team members were at a loss how to react to the gloom that descended on me. For Carlos, Titín, Joan, and Francis Roig, who was with me at Indian Wells instead of Toni, I became a different person, distant and cold; short and sharp in conversation. They worried about me, and they worried about the impact of my parents' separation on my game. They knew I couldn't keep winning; they knew something had to give. And it did. First it was my knees that went.

I felt the first twinges in Miami, at the end of March. The pain got worse week by week, but I managed to keep playing through it until early May, in Madrid, when I couldn't keep going anymore. Mind could no longer overcome matter and I took a break.

I came back a couple of weeks later for the French Open. Maybe I should not have competed in Roland Garros, but I had won the championship the previous four years and I felt a duty to defend my crown, however unlikely the prospect of victory felt. Sure enough, I lost in the fourth round to Robin Soderling of Sweden, my first ever defeat in that tournament. This finally pushed me over the edge. I'd made a huge effort to be in shape for Roland Garros, battling to overcome both my parents' separation and the pain in my knees, but now I knew that, debilitated in mind and body, I could no longer keep going. Terribly sad, I pulled out of Wimbledon, giving up on the chance to defend a title that had been so hard-won, the year before and meant so much to me. My knees were the immediate reason, but I knew that the root cause was my state of mind. My competitive zeal had waned, the adrenaline had dried up. Joan Forcades says there is a "holistic" cause-and-effect connection between emotional distress and physical collapse. He says that if your head is in permanent stress, you sleep little and your mind is distracted—exactly the symptoms I was showing at that time—the impact on your body is devastating. Messages are relayed to the muscles that under the pressure of competition, lead to injuries. I am sure Joan is right.

Being at Wimbledon instead of at home reminded me every minute of how dramatically our lives had been altered, which only deepened my introspection and grief. And while I carried on training with Joan in the gym, gearing the exercises to help my knees recover, the intensity was not there, because the will wasn't. Federer won Wimbledon that year, having won the French Open for the first time a month before, and snatched back the world number one spot from me almost exactly a year after I had taken it away from him. It was a blow, but it would have hurt a lot more under ordinary circumstances. My sense of loss remained centered on what had happened at home.

But I am not a malingerer. If I felt healthy, I would never play truant from the tour. After the Wimbledon break, in early August, I rejoined the circuit in North America, playing first in Toronto and then in Cincinnati. My knees were just about holding up, though I failed to win either tournament, but in Cincinnati I suffered yet another setback. I tore an abdominal muscle. That's not an unusual injury among tennis players. It affects your serve, in particular, as you stretch and twist to strike the ball, but it's something you can play through if you are feeling otherwise well. Next up was the US Open, and this time I didn't pull out. I advanced further, under the circumstances, than I might have expected, falling in the semifinals to Juan del Potro of Argentina, who beat me comfortably— 6–2, 6–2, 6–2—and went on to win the tournament. But that was enough. It was time to call a halt, allow myself time off to face up to the new reality at home, try and learn how to deal with it, take my mind off tennis a little and give my body time to recover.

I've never reached the point of hating tennis, as some professional players say they have. You can't hate something, I don't think, that puts the food on the table and has given you almost everything you have in life. There can come a time, though, when you grow weary and a part of that fanatical enthusiasm you need to keep competing at the highest level begins to ebb. I've always believed, as Toni has, that to keep competing you must never break your established patterns. You have to carry on training hard, long hours whether you feel like it or not, because any slack in intensity will be reflected in your results on court. But a point comes when you just cannot keep going at a hundred percent, mind and body, every single day, and the best thing to do is pause and wait for the desire to return.

By Christmas 2009, eleven months after first learning of the problems in my parents' marriage, we had begun learning to adapt to the new family dynamic. My mother—who'd had a miserable 2009—was recovering her old zest, and I made up my mind that the moment had come to turn over a new leaf. The media were full of stories questioning whether I'd ever return to my best, with some experts even wondering whether my hard physical game had taken a toll from which I'd never fully recover, and this only sharpened my desire to get back and prove the skeptics wrong. Toni, himself not immune to the family traumas, had been sympathetic, for the most part. But now, as my annus horribilis approached its end, he said that enough was enough. It was time to buck up and return to work. "There are a lot of people who have problems in life but keep going," he said. "What makes you so special that you should be the exception?" While blunt, as usual, he had a point. The soreness in my knees never entirely went away, but I resumed full training. As 2010 approached, I battled hard to be in shape for the Australian Open.

I didn't expect to win, but I was bitterly disappointed at the manner of my exit, in the quarter finals, against Andy Murray. I had to pull out halfway through the third set because of my knees. Murray had won the first two sets, and in the spirit of honest competition, I would have liked to keep going to the end, even if it was obvious that victory would be his. But the pain was so bad, and the potential damage to the knees so great, that I had to call a halt. It was another blow after all the hard work I'd done to prepare for Australia, and all the more so when my doctor told me I'd need two weeks of rest and then two weeks of rehabilitation before I could compete again, further evidence that the life you lead as an elite athlete is not good for your health—a point on which Joan Forcades, who in my view is a world expert on the subject, entirely agrees.

The doubters had more ammunition than ever now, but I refused to believe I was down and out. I did not become despondent the way I had five years earlier, when the problem in my tarsal scaphoid bone laid me low. I was able to walk, if not to sprint. I wasn't limping on crutches or hitting balls sitting on a chair.

A month passed and I was back to reasonable fitness, feeling well enough to compete in March in Indian Wells and Miami, where I reached the semifinals both times. And then, once again, it was at Monte Carlo where the breakthrough came. Back on clay, I recovered my old self. I lost only fourteen games in all five matches and beat Fernando Verdasco (who had driven me to tears of despair during that five-hour five set match in the Australian Open), 6–0, 6–1 in the final, making it six Monte Carlo victories in a row. I had another reason to be cheerful. My father and Dr. Cotorro had been hunting for a solution to my knee problems, and it seemed that finally they might have had some luck. I had scheduled a visit straight after Monte Carlo to a medical center in Vitoria, the capital of Spain's Basque Country, where they had a treatment doctors believed could cure me once and for all. It would involve injections without anesthetics to the knees, a prospect that hardly filled me with joy, but I'd do whatever it took to recover full fitness. I'd had this problem for a year now and I wanted it to go away.

Getting to Vitoria, where I had my doctor's appointment on the

Monday after the Sunday of the Monte Carlo final, proved to be more of a challenge than my two companions on the trip, my father and Titín, and I might at first have imagined. The normal thing would have been to go by plane from Nice, via Barcelona. The problem was that practically the whole of Europe's airspace had been closed off due to the eruption of a volcano in Iceland. The prevailing winds were carrying a gigantic ash cloud south, all the way to Spain, and the aviation authorities had canceled all flights due to the risk of the cloud's gritty little particles causing airplane engines to seize up in the air. So we had to travel from Monte Carlo to Victoria by road, a trip of about one thousand kilometers. Our appointment being at noon on Monday, we'd have to drive all through the night. But there was an additional complication. Real Madrid had a big match that Sunday night, and there was simply no question of missing it. So we went to Benito's home (he lives in Monte Carlo), ordered in some pizzas and watched the game, which Real won, and then set off just before midnight, taking turns at the wheel.

We hadn't been on the road long when we realized we were all too tired to drive the whole way without a break. So we phoned Benito and asked him to try and find us a place where we could stop and snatch a few hours of sleep. Benito got on the case, calling a modest roadside hotel in Narbonne, in southern France, about a third of the way along our route. Benito is a persuasive man, but he had a struggle convincing the night receptionist that this wasn't a crank call, that—yes, no kidding—Rafa Nadal and party would indeed be needing rooms there at three thirty in the morning.

We got up a few hours later, having slept too little and hardly in the mood for the remaining seven hours of driving that still lay ahead. Luckily, we were able to push back the appointment with the doctor to the afternoon, which allowed us to break up the journey a little.

The injections, without anesthetic, were as painful as I had expected them to be. As the doctor jabbed me, I bit a towel, needing to believe that the treatment would achieve its objective: to allow the knee's tendons to regenerate and strengthen to such a degree that the problem would not just go away now, it would never come back.

After another obligatory period of rest, I was back two weeks later for the Rome Masters tournament. I felt distinctly better, despite the knowledge that I'd have to return to Vitoria for another round of injections in July. I won in Rome and then I won in Madrid, silencing quite a lot of the talk of my imminent tennis death en route to the big test of whether my resurrection was complete: the French Open. I had not won a Grand Slam tournament since Melbourne, nearly a year and a half earlier, but I entered this one as the favorite.

This worried Toni, who always fretted at the prospect of success going to my head. This has become a reflex for him, taken sometimes to ludicrous extremes. One day early on in the French Open he and I were strolling side by side with Carlos Costa down a wide Paris sidewalk. I was walking in the middle, with Toni and Carlos on either side. Suddenly Toni stopped, "Wait a minute. We can't have this." Carlos and I looked at him, puzzled and mildly irritated, as if to say, "What now?" "We can't have this!" he said. "Can't have what?" "You, Rafael, walking in the middle like that." In Toni's mind we were conveying the message to passersby that I was the special one of the three, as if he and Carlos were my bodyguards, or courtiers. Carlos, who is less patient with Toni than I am, began to remonstrate. "For heaven's sake, Toni . . ." But my attitude in moments like these is "anything for a bit of peace." So I succumbed to Toni's whim and took my place on the outside of our threesome, as he wished.

The more important objective I achieved in Paris was to silence the doomsday critics once and for all. I lived up to my billing as favorite, not dropping a set on the way to the final, where I met Robin Soderling, who had knocked me out of the French Open the year before. Soderling had beaten Federer in the quarter finals, and this meant that if I beat Soderling I'd have gathered sufficient points to reclaim the number one spot in the world rankings. And I did, winning the final in straight sets, 6–4, 6–2, 6–4, and notching my seventh Grand Slam.

Wimbledon was the next big one, a month later. Having not even taken part the year before, having felt so miserable then, I had a special desire to get back and win my second victory. I felt confident I would. Carlos Costa says I am like a diesel engine. I don't always set off very fast, but once I get going, I'm unstoppable. That might be a slight exaggeration, but it was true that right now, June 2010, the momentum was with me again.

The fact that things had settled on the parental front, freeing my head to concentrate on my tennis once again, had made all the difference. The devastating impact the separation had had on me demonstrated, conclusively, the umbilical connection between stability in my family circle and stability in my tennis game. The circuits were too intimately interconnected for one not to affect the other. But time had passed—nearly a year and a half now since my father had broken the news to me on the way back from Melbourne— and I had reprogrammed myself to adjust to the new realities. Thanks to my parents, these had not turned out to be as destructive as I might initially have feared. They remained apart, but they had handled things well, making the continued well-being of my sister and me paramount. Some couples who separate try to use their children as instruments of vengeance on each other. It was quite the opposite in my parents' case. They each did what they could to soften the blow for Maribel and me. After the inevitable initial acrimony, there had been no nastiness, and in time, they even became friends again, to the extent that they started coming along together again to tournaments to watch me play. There are civilized and uncivilized separations. This one has been civilized, and I admire and love them for that.

And so it was that on the morning after winning the French Open, in a cheerful frame of mind after a night of celebration at a party with Beyoncé and other celebrities, I found myself heading to Disneyland Paris with my father, Titín, Benito, and Tuts. We had a prearranged photo shoot there. Despite the lack of sleep, it was a professional obligation I had no problem fulfilling. I'd been to Disneyland Paris before, and I'd always had a great time there. I love being in the company of children; I connect with them naturally and well.

The bad news was that we went by helicopter, a form of transport I have to take sometimes but which always terrifies me. We survived the ride, which added to my enjoyment of the rides I took on some of the attractions, and allowed me to smile easily for the cameras when the time came to pose alongside Goofy and Mr. and Mrs. Incredible with my French Open trophy. And then it was straight back to central Paris to catch the train to London.

The Queen's Tournament, the prelude to Wimbledon, is played on grass. It began in a week, and I wanted to get in some practice on this surface as soon as possible. So after we emerged from under the English Channel and arrived, an hour or so later, at the railway station in London, we headed straight for the Queen's Club instead of the hotel. It was raining, as it so often is in London, and so I had to wait in the locker room along with some other players, among them Andy Roddick, for the sun to return. There wasn't much to do there except stare at a TV screen where, as it happened, they were showing a rerun of my 2008 Wimbledon final against Roger Federer. The rest of the players were as engrossed as I was, but we hadn't got far into the match before I realized that the rain had stopped. I jumped up. "God! Come on! Let's go out and train!" I said to Titín. My companions in the locker room, who were still watching my match, looked at me in amazement, as if they thought I should be sitting down and savoring my famous victory instead of showing such eagerness to get out on court. But, for me, there was not a second to waste. After nearly two years away, I had to get back the feel of playing on grass right away.

I had won Queen's in 2008 but lost in the quarterfinals this time around. This was no catastrophe as it gave me more time to prepare at my own pace for Wimbledon. I moved out of my hotel in London and returned to our English home away from home, the rental house next door to the All England Club. It was good to be back. Just as my absence from Wimbledon 2009 had signified how shaken up I was by the disruption in my family life, so my coming back in 2010 meant a return to calm.

That diesel engine image Carlos Costa uses to describe me was especially appropriate in this tournament. I started off sluggishly, but once I got going, there was no stopping me. I nearly went out in the second round, squeaking through in five sets, but the further I advanced, and the tougher the opponents were—by ranking, at any rate—the more my game improved. I beat Soderling in the quarterfinals in four sets and Andy Murray in the semis in three. In the match against Murray the Centre Court crowd behaved impeccably. The British have been longing to have their own Wimbledon champion since 1936, when Fred Perry last won, and the crowd made it quite clear from the start where their allegiances lay. Murray, seeded four in the tournament, was the best hope they had had in a long time. Yet I felt they were entirely fair with me throughout, not cheering my double faults, clapping after my better shots. And when, to the disappointment of the great majority, I won in straight sets, they did not begrudge me a warm round of applause.

I had expected that if I made it to the final, I'd be meeting Roger Federer for the fourth year running. I didn't. My opponent this time was the number twelve seed Tomas Berdych, of the Czech Republic, who'd had a brilliant run in the tournament, beating Federer in the quarters and Djokovic in the semifinals. Though complacency was the last thing on my mind, I was not nearly as nervous as I had been before the final two years earlier. Just as never having played a Wimbledon final before places you at a disadvantage, the experience of having done so—in my case four times now—provides a soothing measure of familiarity. Playing an almost perfect game, I won in three sets, 6–3, 7–5, 6–4, to collect my second Wimbledon championship and eighth Grand Slam.

The game ended early, but I didn't get any sleep that night. After the official Wimbledon dinner, where I had to wear a tuxedo and dance, as protocol requires, with the ladies' winner, Serena Williams, there was no point in going to bed. The event ended after midnight, and I only had two and a half hours before I had to leave for the airport with my father and Titín. We were taking a dawn flight on a low-cost airline to Bilbao, from where we'd drive to Vitoria, an hour away, for the second and decisive round of injections to my knee. We could have scheduled the treatment for later, but I wanted to get back to Mallorca as soon as possible for the summer break I always take after Wimbledon. People say that the homing instinct is particularly strong among islanders. This is powerfully true in my case. When the urge to return home comes over me, sleep is no consideration.

As it turned out, there had been no need for such an early start. The doctor judged that this was not the best time to inject me, because there was some reason to fear the knee might become infected. So we turned swiftly back to Bilbao and flew to Palma, returning later to Vitoria for the treatment, which has been very successful. My knee problems are gone. I took a rest, a longer one than I usually do in the summer, having judged that this was what I needed to be best prepared for the one big remaining challenge that awaited me: completing the foursome of Grand Slams by winning the US Open.

I took three weeks off from tennis and this time not because of injury or because I was emotionally distraught, but for the more positive reason that the moment had come to press the reset button. I wanted to draw a line between the on-court and off-court tensions of the previous year and a half before starting again with a clean slate. I went fishing, swam in the sea, played golf, went clubbing with my friends, often very late into the night, and spent time with María Francisca. It was a relief, for a while at least, not to be constantly besieged by journalists, or to appear in the newspapers every day. It was liberating not to have to mix with the same players day in, day out in the locker rooms and club restaurants, or to watch my rivals' matches on TV, or to drive from hotels to tennis clubs to hotels again to train or play, sometimes losing track when I woke up in the morning of what city I was in. I handle all this well, and I accept that it goes with the territory, but like everyone with a job, I need a vacation from time to time. In what I do for a living, the risk of burnout is high. I figured that if I were to have a chance of winning the US Open, the most important thing at this stage was to cleanse my mind so that when the time came to resume play I'd do so with the necessary hunger and enthusiasm.

It wasn't until early August, ten days before the start of my North

American summer tour, that I resumed full training. That was a record. The minimum I had previously allowed myself before a tournament was fifteen days' preparation. This time ten days felt right. It was not enough to win in Toronto, where I lost in the semifinals, or in Cincinnati, where I didn't make it past the quarterfinals. But, while I didn't play especially well in those competitions, I had a feeling in my gut that the best was yet to come. Sometimes it's better not to arrive for a Grand Slam firing on all cylinders, because there's the risk that if you fail to sustain your best level in the opening matches, you'll become disappointed with yourself and morale will fade.

The calculations proved to be right, in the end, although at first I wasn't so sure. I started out a little hesitantly at Flushing Meadow, in part because of a spat with Toni that brought to the boil the long accumulated tensions between us. It had to do with something he had been badgering me about ever since we had started out together two decades earlier: the need, while competing, to put on what in Spanish we call *una buena cara*, "a good face."

To have a good face means to wear a serious, concentrated expression when you are playing, one that betrays as few negative emotions as possible, reflecting an attitude of persistence and professional discipline. The opposite of a good face is one that reflects the rage, the nerves, the tension, the fear, or even the elation you might be feeling. As Toni sees it, this is not merely a question of esthetics or good manners. The theory, and Joan Forcades agrees with Toni on this, is that the expression on your face conditions to a significant degree your state of mind and, in the case of a tennis player, the functioning of your body. In other words, if you manage to keep a good face during a match, the better the chances are that you won't be distracted by the shot you just hit, be it good or bad, or the point you just lost or won, focusing all your mind instead on the present, on the immediate necessities of the job at hand. It's another way of putting into practice Toni's principle of endurance, and it's another aspect of what Joan calls the "holistic" approach necessary to succeed in elite sports.

And, by and large, I agree with them. That is why I do always endeavor to present a good face to the world, as I did, I think, consistently during the Wimbledon Final of 2008. It is no accident that my proudest recollection of that match is the attitude I displayed from start to finish. So, yes, Toni is right. Keeping a good face gives you a competitive edge in tennis. But I am not perfect and I cannot always disguise my feelings. And it was because I failed to do so, according to Toni, during my second-round match in the 2010 US Open, against Denis Istomin of Uzbekistan, that we had our quarrel—a quite needless quarrel, in my view, that he precipitated and that could have had a damaging impact on the rest of my New York campaign.

This is what happened. Before that second-round match began, Toni had said to me I should play safe, hit high balls, stretch out the points, concentrate on getting my rhythm going for the tougher games that lay ahead. I did exactly as he said and I won. But I wasn't playing at my best, and I imagine my face must have reflected a certain anxiety. In the locker room after the match, Toni complained that I had not played with a good face, that my attitude had been poor. I disagreed and said, "I don't understand why you react this way when I played exactly as you told me to. And I don't know why you feel the need to reproach me in this way when the majority of people only have praise for my attitude on court. If my face looks the way you said it does, it's because I was feeling nervous, because I was afraid I might lose, which I think is an entirely understandable human reaction. But my concentration was good during the whole match and, anyway, I won. So what's the big deal?"

"OK," he said. "OK. I just tell you what I think, and if you don't like it, I'm off home and you can go find yourself another coach."

I wasn't thrilled at his reaction. Toni must know that I am one of the easiest players on the tour to get on with. Few treat their coach with more respect than I do. I listen to Toni, I do as he instructs, and even when things between us become tense, I rarely answer back. I am well mannered on court, I train at a hundred percent, and in everyday life I don't put any pressure on those around me, much less Toni. So when he responded the way he did that day in the locker room at Flushing Meadows, I felt I was being treated unjustly. But I made an effort and contained myself.

"Look," I said, "you always say the same thing. And usually I agree with you. But this time—this time—I believe you're wrong."

He wouldn't listen. "Fine," said Toni. "If this is the way things are going to be, I can't see any pleasure in being your coach any longer." And, on that note, he stormed out of the locker room.

It got me thinking. There's a fine balance in the tension that my uncle's presence in my life creates. Usually, as the record shows, it's been a positive, creative tension. Sometimes, and this was a case in point, he doesn't measure his words well and the effect is to sour, rather than to enhance, my mood, which in turn impacts my game. A trivial example of the sort of thing I have to put up with would be this: We are at a hotel somewhere in the world and we agree to meet downstairs in the car at a certain time to go to training. He arrives fifteen minutes late, but I don't say anything. But the next time I arrive fifteen minutes late for an appointment, he complains that we can't carry on this way.

Another example. During a match I'll hear him say, "Play aggressive!" before a return of serve, meaning he wants me to hit the ball back hard. I'll go for it, the ball will go out, and then he'll say, "Now wasn't the moment." But it was the moment; it just happened that I messed up the shot. If the ball had gone in, he'd have said, "Perfect!"

And there's another thing, a story he told a reporter during the US Open about a little incident that had happened one night five years earlier in an elevator in Shanghai. We were heading down for dinner when Benito pointed out that the dress code in the restaurant insisted that long pants be worn. I was wearing shorts, but Benito said, "Oh, don't worry. Being who you are, they are not going to cause a fuss." Toni, as he told the story, replied to Benito, "Fine example you're setting for my nephew!" And then, turning to me, he said, "Go upstairs and get changed."

Now, I'm not denying those were the words that were spoken, more or less. But the truth of that story is that I did not need Toni to tell me I had to go back to my room to get changed. I had made up my mind I would the moment Benito pointed out what the restaurant's rules were.

Incidents like these mean that the atmosphere in our team is tenser when Toni's around than when he's not. What I never lose sight of is that, on balance, that tension benefits my game. Nor do I forget that he wouldn't generate such a response in me, be it for good or for bad, if I didn't feel a tremendous respect for him. When I am hard on him, it's because I believe he asks for it. But one thing must be clear: If we have fights, they are to be taken in the context of a mutual trust and a deep affection built up over many years of being together. I do not begrudge him the public recognition he has. He may have obtained it due to me, but everything I have achieved in the game of tennis, all the opportunities I have had, are thanks to him. I'm especially grateful to him for having placed so much emphasis from the very beginning on making sure I kept my feet on the ground and never became complacent.

I don't think success has gone to my head, and if it hasn't yet, I doubt it will happen now. I don't need these lessons in humility anymore. I don't need to be told anymore that I have "to put on a good face." If I mess up sometimes on court, well, it's part of the game. I am as critical of myself as anybody. While Toni's refusal to let me off the hook has its value, in that he pushes me always to improve and do better, it can also be bad because he creates insecurity. I often do feel this way, especially in the early rounds of a tournament, and the truth is that while he deserves credit for so many good things in my career, he also deserves blame for me being more insecure than I ought to be.

The joke is that lately he's taken to saying that I have a tendency to underestimate myself. He says this is crazy given everything I've achieved. Before a match against an opponent who is way down the rankings, he'll say to me now, "After all you've done you're not going to get yourself into a fret over this game, are you?" Or he'll say, "You've been number one or number two for years now, yet you're still not convinced you're a good player? You're still afraid when you go up against the guy who's ranked 120? To strut around like you own the game would be stupid, but come on, you've got to learn to know who you are!" The trouble with having this exaggerated sense of respect for all my opponents, he says, is that then on court my arm tightens up and I play beneath myself. And he's right. Of course he's right. But he's the one who put in the software in the first place; the way he's worked on me during all these years has influenced me to have precisely the opposite attitude to the one he demands of me now.

The point now is to hold on to the lessons I've absorbed from Toni but to impose my own judgment more, striving to find the right balance between humility and overconfidence. Sure, you must always respect your rival, always consider the possibility that he might beat you, always play against the player ranked 500 in the world as if he were ranked number one or two. Toni has helped me to have this very clear in my mind, maybe too clear. What I am trying to teach myself now is to tilt the balance the other way, to exercise more autonomy over my life and disagree more openly with Toni, as I did at the start of the US Open. This may be a consequence, in part, of me seeing that Toni has his doubts and insecurities too; that he contradicts himself often; that he is not the all-knowing magician of my childhood.

We patched up that scuffle in the locker room. We made up as we always do. We need each other, and as we both knew, with the prospect of a fourth Grand Slam around the corner, this was hardly the moment for another family split. The pattern in my life has been that I've emerged stronger from the crises I've endured, large and small. I began playing better and better in the US Open after that, and by the time I got to the final against Djokovic, I felt in top shape. My forehand, great all year, was rock solid during that first set; the backhand, perfectly solid; the serve, the best it had ever been.

That did not stop me going 4–1 down in the second set. But that was more because he suddenly hit a patch in which every shot he went for worked out, than because I was going off my game. I knew he couldn't sustain that level of play, and I felt I deserved better. And it was in that confident frame of mind that I broke his serve, saving a point that would have given him a 5–2 lead, and then went on to pull the score back to 4–4.

I was on the upswing now, and he appeared to be discouraged at having lost his big chance to clinch the set, when, at 30–30 on his serve, the rain came. The early sunshine had given way to ever darker clouds, and I had seen streaks of lightning in the distance. The umpire stopped play, and the tournament referee came on court, telling us "I'm afraid this is going to be a nasty one." He was right. We heard thunder from deep down in the locker room, where we remained for two hours, before reemerging to resume play at eight o'clock.

The break had suited Djokovic more than it had me, just as it had Roger Federer that first time we went off for rain in Wimbledon two years earlier. I'd had the momentum and Djokovic had needed time to collect himself. He did, winning the interrupted game to go 5–4 up. I held my serve and then he, his, and once again I served to save the set at 6–5 down.

I won the first point with a sharply angled forehand drive that he could do nothing about, and he got a bit of luck to win the next one, when my shot hit the net cord but, instead of dribbling over, dropped on my side. That turned out to be the story of the set. I think I played as well as he did, probably better, controlling more points than he, putting him permanently on the back foot and obliging him to hustle more than to attack. That was a role I was more accustomed to playing, but he performed it well, retrieving some shots he had no right to, and won the set 7–5, the first one I had lost in the entire tournament.

The rain had proved a blessing for him. At Wimbledon in 2008 it had turned out, in the end, to be a blessing for me. With the match tied at one set all, it was back to the beginning. We'd have to wait and see whether the gods of tennis would smile on me once more.

RAFA'S WOMEN

RAFA NADAL HAS three women in his life: his mother, his sister, and his girlfriend. They all share what his mother, Ana María Parera, calls "a doctrine" for how to conduct themselves in the world. The idea, as simple as it is unusual in the light of Rafa's global celebrity, is best summed up for her by the most unexciting, unglamorous word in the dictionary: "normality."

Excitement and glamour are what the public sees in Rafa Nadal; what Ana María sees is a son who, when he leaves home, dwells in a world of chaos. Her duty as a mother is to be his anchor of stability, to create a safe haven for him from the bombardment on all fronts that he has endured since becoming, at what she regards as an alarmingly tender age, one of the most famous and admired athletes the world has known.

This has meant shunning the media spotlight and relating to her son as if there were nothing remarkable in what he has achieved, an example followed by her daughter, Maribel, and by Rafa's girlfriend since 2005, María Francisca Perelló. Each, in theory, could have made another choice. Ana María could have made a career out of blabbing to the world about her son's inner feelings and foibles. Maribel, a tall and attractive blonde, could have become a rumor-mongering staple of gossip magazines. María Francisca could have become almost as recognizable a global personage as Rafa himself.

They have not chosen these paths because they know it is the last thing in the world Rafa himself desires or needs, because they are not prey to the insecurities that Ana María believes underlie the celebrity-craving camp followers of the rich and famous, and because it is not their style. They are all from Manacor, and Manacor people by nature and culture keep themselves to themselves, are wary of strangers.

"I've always been very discreet about my private things," Ana María says. "If anything, Rafael's fame has made me even more discreet, more protective of our life at home. I don't like to confide in people I don't know. There are those who crave popularity, who in my situation might love to talk and talk about their son, bask in his reflected glory. But that's not me. Inside, I am enormously proud of him and so happy at all the success he's had, but I don't advertise my feelings. I don't even talk about him to my closest friends."

She has had a hint in her own life, a small taste, of what it means to be famous. She is recognized sometimes on the streets of Barcelona, London, or New York by people who have glimpsed her on television watching her son at big tournaments. And not only does she feel uncomfortable when strangers approach her, she is struck by a crushingly claustrophobic sense of how relentlessly under siege her son is when he steps out into the wide world beyond Manacor.

"The only place where anything resembling intimacy is possible while he is away on tour is inside his hotel rooms, the only hiding places he has. He can't walk down a street without creating a commotion. The media and his sponsors make constant claims on him. And then there's the incredible tension of competition, the insecurities and fears I know he has to battle to control during the week or two weeks that tournaments last in order to keep winning and stay at the top. He is my son, and it frightens and amazes me to see how strong he has to be, how strong he is."

He would not be as strong without the respite that home provides. Home is where Rafa Nadal comes up for air. And the center and symbol of home is his mother, especially following his parents' separation, when his father moved out. Sebastián Nadal accompanies him much more frequently than Ana María does on his international campaigns, providing a pillar of support everywhere he goes. He has become as intimately associated with Rafa's tennis life as the professional team around him. Ana María inhabits a world in which high-powered tennis competitions, and the commercial and media commitments that have gone hand-in-hand with Rafa's standing as world number one, are marginal concerns. She barely talks to her son about his professional life, not because she is not interested but because she knows that the best favor she can do him is engage with him as any other mother would with any other son. She is not in awe of his accomplishments on the tennis court, in his guise as the globally acclaimed "Rafa Nadal," but treats him with the easy tenderness and devotion she feels for him as the Rafael she gave birth to and fed and raised. She is his antidote to adulation, grounding him and reminding him of who he really is.

"But the most important thing, now that I see fame has not gone to his head, and never will, is to make him feel at peace when he is home," Ana María says. "He needs peace because that is the last thing he has when he is away on tour, but also because of the way he is, irrespective of the madness surrounding his life. He's always had a terrible time when the people around him are angry or in a bad temper; he gets angry or bad-tempered too. Emotionally, he needs everything to be perfectly in order around him.

"That is why I see it as my duty when we are together to do everything I can, as any other mother would, to see to it that he is happy and well and, when he is not happy and well, to be there to support him. And supporting him—for example, when he's been injured—often means saying nothing, just making it clear that I am there for him, whatever the circumstances. It means he can feel at ease when he's home; that he can invite his friends around any time he wants without me making any demands on him. And if he needs me to drive him somewhere, or buy him something to eat that he craves, or pack his suitcase for him before a long trip— something he is disastrously incapable of doing on his own, by the way—I'll do it, happily."

Ana María's living room is a social hub for Rafa's friends when he is back home. Chief among his friends, ever present on nights out or on fishing trips, is his sister, Maribel. She is five years younger than he is, and he adores her and misses her badly when he is away, although they keep in constant contact by phone and the Internet. Maribel is aware of the fact that her connection with her brother is unusually close, remarking that many of her friends' relationships with their younger siblings tend to be marked either by friction or benign neglect. "Most boys growing up see their younger sisters as irritations, especially when they are teenagers," she says. "But that has never been the way Rafael has treated me. He's always urged me to come along when he goes out with his friends. It's natural to us, even if others might sometimes find it strange, and it's part of the secret of our special bond."

Ana María believes that another reason why her two children are so close is that they have spent so much time away from each other ever since Rafa ventured off in his early teens to conquer the tennis world. They do not take each other for granted, and absence, she thinks, has made the heart grow fonder. This may not have been the case if Maribel had allowed his fame go to her head. Instead, she has followed her mother's cue. "If anything, she has been even more discreet than I have," Ana María says, pointing to the fact that it was not until two years into her university course in Barcelona, where Maribel is studying sports education, that anyone outside her closest circle of friends had any idea who her brother was. "Word only got around after one of her lecturers spotted her on TV during a tennis match Rafael was playing in Paris."

María Francisca has had to work harder to preserve her anonymity. Not so much because of her courtside appearances, which are infrequent (the first Grand Slam final she watched him play in was Wimbledon 2010), but because the paparazzi have not been able to resist the temptation to photograph her and Rafa together when they are on vacation, preferably on a beach. She has seen herself splashed across the pages of celebrity gossip magazines more times than she would care to count. Yet she is never quoted saying anything. As a perplexed commentator on Spanish TV observed five years into the couple's relationship, no one had ever heard her speak. She is such an enigma that neither the TV shows nor the magazines have even been able to get her name right. She has been introduced to the public, worldwide, as Xisca (pronounced "Chisca"), yet no one she knows calls her by that name. Rafa addresses her by the nickname "Mary," as do some of his family, but to everybody else she remains, simply, María Francisca.

All the public know of her is that she is an elegant, seemingly demure young woman and, as a consequence, the media, for lack of anything else to go on, typically describe her as "serious," "distant," "modest," and, even, "mysterious." It would be hard to imagine anyone further removed from the brash stereotype of the celebrity-seeking WAG—a term coined in the UK for the "wives and girl-friends" of rich and famous sportsmen. The truth is that, while she is loyal to Rafa and experiences his victories and defeats as if they were her own, she treasures her independence and does not wish to be defined in terms of her relationship with him. She has a degree in business administration and has a full-time job with an insur-ance company in Palma, the Mallorcan capital. This means that she does not have the time to follow Rafa around the world, which she would not want to do even if she did. "Traveling together everywhere, even if I could, would not be good either for him or for me. He needs his space when he is competing, and just the idea of me hanging around waiting on his needs all day wears me out. It would asphyxiate me. And then he would have to be worrying about me . . . No. If I followed him everywhere, I think there's a risk we might stop getting along."

When she does accompany him to a tournament, usually when Ana María and Maribel also go along, she goes out of her way to be seen in public with him as little as possible. She remembers a time when they were in Paris and he had to go to a dinner hosted by one of his sponsors. "He asked me if I wanted to go, but I chose not to," she says. "I stayed in our hotel. When Rafael got back he said, 'Thank God you didn't come.' The place had been swarming with photographers. For me to have gone would have meant step-ping into that celebrity world. It's not a world I want to be part of, nor do I think Rafa would have chosen to be with a woman who looked for that in life."

Ana María, who approves warmly of María Francisca's desire to carve out a separate working life of her own, agrees that Rafa could not possibly have a sustained a relationship with a woman who hungered for media attention. Nor can she imagine, she says, a woman with more equanimity and good humor, or better suited by temperament to her son. She and María Francisca are fast friends, as are Maribel and María Francisca, the three of them bonded not only by their love for Rafa, but by their shared attachment to Ana María's normality "doctrine." "Even if my family asks me about Rafael, I prefer not to say much," says María Francisca, who echoes Ana María's words, and Maribel's sentiments, when she adds: "The fact is that I just don't feel comfortable talking about these things, even in private. It's what works for me, and what works for Rafael and me as a couple. We wouldn't have it any other way."

CHAPTER 9

ON TOP OF THE WORLD

THE SECRET LIES in being able to do what you know you can do when you most need it. Djokovic is a fantastic player—more naturally gifted than I am, in Toni's view—but in a Grand Slam final, decided over the best of five sets, nerves and stamina count as much as talent. Any doubts I might have had before the match began had been dispelled by my performance in the first two sets. As for the stress of a US Open final, I'd won eight Grand Slams to his one, and that gave me the confidence of knowing that I could take it on at least as well as he. Another thing going for me was that his track record showed that he flagged physically in longer matches. He had never beaten me in a best-of-five match. He was, it was true, a player who had dazzling moments, but I was playing steadily, the diesel engine was purring. I sensed that if I won the third set, he'd be left feeling as if he had a mountain to climb.

But he got right into his groove at the start of the third set, picking up where he had left off at the end of the second. The match could not have been more evenly balanced at this point, with the tide, if anything, shifting slightly his way. I shot a glance at my team and family, who were all sitting together in a clump to my left. Toni, Carlos, Titín, my father, and Tuts, and behind them my mother, my sister Maribel, and María Francisca, who looked especially nervous. This was only the second time she'd come to watch me play a Grand Slam final. Usually she watches at home, alone, as she did during Wimbledon in 2008, or with her parents. If it all gets too much for her, she's confessed to me, she changes channels for a while or leaves the room. This time, in New York, she said she had to resist the urge at times to get up and leave. Right now was the moment in the match where her resolve was most tested.

María Francisca has played tennis and understood as well as I did that the rain break had given Djokovic a boost. He showed it in the first point of the set, playing it impeccably, pulling me wide to the left and finishing it off with an electric backhand winner down the line to my right. He repeated the trick, with a deeper shot, after a longer rally on the second point. Too good.

I took it well. Some players explode with anger when their opponent is dominating them. But there's no point. It can only do you harm. You just have to think, "I can't do anything about this, so why worry?" He was taking a lot of risks and they were paying off, for now, but I was managing to play at the level of intensity I wanted, hitting the ball hard and deep without taking risks, leaving myself more margin for error. "Weather the storm," I said to myself. "If I can't come back on the next point, I will on the one after that."

Not in this game, though. He won it, handing me just the one point with a rather inexplicable double fault—he seemed to want to go for a second-serve ace—when he was 40-love up. OK. So it goes. Bad luck. He was ahead, and I'd have to play catch-up on my serve, maybe for a long time.

The next game was a critically important one for me to win. He'd won the previous three, if you included the last two of the second set, and I had to stop him in his tracks or risk being overrun. I played the first point intelligently, playing the ball high. If you hit it low or medium height to Djokovic, especially when his line of vision is as sharp as it was now, he strikes the ball perfectly. But if he receives the ball at shoulder height, you make him uncomfortable, you make him guess, put him off his stride. This was how I went 15–love up. Not by hitting a winner, but by bludgeoning him into making an uncharacteristic mistake. That gave me the confidence to up my game, take a risk, and win the next point with a deep forehand to the corner. He nodded, as if to say, "There was nothing I could do about that." I don't do that. I don't show my appreciation of an opponent's better shots. Not because I am impolite but because it would be too dangerous a departure from my match script. But his attitude was the correct one: bow before the inevitable and move on.

I won the game without dropping a point and then, in an unexpected early bonus, broke his serve to go 2–1 up after playing one of my best shots of the match, a cross-court backhand on the run from two meters behind the base line. He'd gone to the net, quite sensibly, as his approach shot had gone deep to my backhand corner, but I lashed the ball past him before he could even attempt to reach for the volley. I celebrated, piston punching the air, shouting *"Vamos!"* to myself. "Come on!" I had broken Djokovic's momentum, regained the initiative, and shown myself—and him—that I could hit geometrically implausible winners too.

Feeling psychologically at my strongest in the match so far, I felt I was beginning to edge ahead in the mental battle. In our past encounters Djokovic had shown a tendency to grow frustrated as the game progressed when he saw he had to push himself to the limit on every point. He also tended to tire more quickly than I do. That's what I had in the back of my mind. In the front, I was only thinking of the next point.

After the flurry of the third game, it was time to consolidate, capitalize on the break of serve. I'm making calculations all the time as I play, trying to judge the best tactic considering how I am feeling at a given moment, my sense of the opponent's morale, and how the score is going. What I had to do now, I figured, was be patient, keep the rallies going, not force things, seize my chances when they came but not go looking for them. I had to try and tire Djokovic and prey on his nerves, wait for him to make mistakes. That was precisely the pattern of the long first point of the fourth game, which I won. Here I picked up another clue as to his state of mind from his reluctance to go for winners on a couple of balls that I had dropped invitingly short. My confidence grew as his seemed, for the moment, to wane. I won the game at love on my serve to go 3–1 up, sensing I'd have a chance now to break him again.

The chance came, when he went 15–40 down on his serve. I wasn't doing anything special, just concentrating on returning the ball deep, varying the pace of my shots, mixing forehand top spin with backhand back spin, frustrating him, waiting for him to lose his patience. Which he was. But now, with his back against the wall, Djokovic changed tactics. He had been losing the long rallies, so he began approaching the net behind his serve. It worked the first time. He won the next point with a volley. I chose to read his newfound boldness as a sign of desperation, but a big serve brought him back to deuce. Then I got another break point, but I lost it and was angry with myself. Not because I had hit the shot wide but because I had taken too great a risk, sought out too fine an angle when the right tactic now, quite clearly, was not to force things but to keep the ball in play. I'd had a momentary loss of concentration and despised myself for it. He was showing some hesitancy now, but at any moment he could recover his best game and I was wasting my opportunity to build an unassailable lead in the set. And I did waste it. I failed to capitalize on three break points that landed in my lap in the fifth game, while he won the first one that came his way.

But the trend remained favorable for me. He was battling to hold his serve; I was winning mine comfortably—as I did now, at love, to go 4–2 up. Another chance to break him and what felt like another thousand game points to me, but again I failed to make the decisive breakthrough. I was playing better, undoubtedly, and he was on the ropes—but holding on. We each held serve the next two games, and I found myself serving at 5–4 for the set.

Now I became nervous. It is when victory appears to be in sight that I so often seem to suffer an attack of vertigo. If I won the game and I went two sets to one up, I'd be two thirds of the way to winning my fourth Grand Slam. Djokovic would then have to win the next two sets, and he could see that I wouldn't be giving him an inch. Much as I tried to banish the thought entirely from my mind, there it lurked, inhibiting me. That was why it was important to keep playing safe, sticking more than ever to my natural defensive game, hoping his nerves would be more frayed than mine.

We started out the game with two very long rallies, more than twenty shots each. I won the first one when he hit the ball long; he, the second, with a terrific forehand winner. It was fifteen all and I felt the tension rise, yet I remained just about composed enough to register that, satisfied as he might have been at having won the point so well, he also grasped he'd have to dig very deep to get the upper hand against me. He'd have been thinking, "Oooof! What a lot of work I need to do to get a point off this guy!" What I was seeing, meanwhile, was that he was tired and panting hard, and I thought, "I doubt whether he'll be able to pull off a shot like that in a hurry again." Or that's what I wanted to believe, at any rate.

I lost the next point with a reckless forehand but bounced back to 30–30 with a great serve high and wide. Typically, I would have played safe on the serve. I'd have concentrated on getting the first one in, sparing myself the prospect of handing him the possible gift of a hesitant second serve. But I'd never been more confident in my serve than in this tournament, and I felt the moment had come to go for broke. It was the correct decision. My next serve was an ace, which gave me set point, and the one after that was just as good—wide, hard, and unreturnable on his backhand side. I had won the set 6–4.

Here was crystal clear vindication of the philosophy of hard work that had guided me in my twenty years of tennis life. Here was compelling cause-and-effect evidence that the will to win and the will to prepare are one and the same. I had worked long and hard before the US Open on my serve. And here it was, paying off when I most needed it, saving me at just the moment when my nerves threatened to undermine the rest of my game. I was on the brink of something truly great. The fact that I had got to this point was the culmination of long years of sacrifice and dedication, all based on the unbreakable premise that there are no shortcuts to sustained success. You can't cheat in elite sports. Talent alone won't get you through. That's just the first building block, on top of which you must pile relentlessly repetitive work in the gym, work on the courts, work studying videos of yourself and your opponents in action, always striving to get fitter, better, cleverer. I made a choice to become a professional tennis player, and the result of that choice could only be unflagging discipline and a continual desire to improve.

Had I sat back after winning the French Open, or Wimbledon, believing my game to be complete enough to guarantee further success, I would not have been here now at Arthur Ashe Stadium in New York with a chance of adding the US Open to my list of conquests. I'd made it as far as I had because I had never lost sight of my priorities. The real test comes on those mornings when you wake up after a late night out and the very last thing you want to do is get up and train, knowing you're going to work furiously hard and you're going to sweat buckets. There might be a moment's debate in your mind. "Should I skip it today, just this once?" But you don't listen to your mind's siren songs because you know that they will lead you down a dangerously steep and slippery slope. If you flag once, you'll flag again.

Occasionally, deeper doubts have assailed me. After spending Christmas with my family in Mallorca, when I take a month off from competition, I find myself contemplating the start of the new year in a contradictory frame of mind. The enthusiasm I feel is undercut by a sense of gloom. I want to climb new mountains, but they remain mountains. I know only too well how remorselessly, grindingly demanding the year ahead is going to be. On all fronts: training, travel, competition, the requests from the media, the sponsors, the fans. And the majority of my time will be spent so far from home, the place where I always want to be. It is with a heavy heart, often, that I board my first flight of the year, heading east, en route to Australia. Once we've taken off, the gloom lifts and I turn my attention fully, with mounting excitement, to the task at hand. But I have a personal life beyond tennis, and winning the battle between my private needs and the demands of my profession is another element of success on the court. But sometimes it is a battle I wish I didn't have to fight.

My sister, Maribel, remembers a time three or four years ago when she came into our home and found me sitting on the stairs weeping. I was in the last stages of recovery from an injury and preparing to rejoin the tennis tour. She asked me what the matter was, and I told her that all of a sudden I'd been filled with a terrible sense of regret at having denied myself the opportunity to spend more time playing with my friends when I was a child. My sister was surprised. Ninety percent of the time at home, save for that period after our parents' separation, we laugh and joke together. And never had I expressed such a thought to her before. But that moment of despondency revealed, however fleetingly, my understanding that I had indeed made a lot of sacrifices to get where I am today, that there had been a cost.

Yet there had never really been any choice in the matter. The dominant part of my nature had been revealed in that other episode years earlier when, at the age of ten, I had wept bitterly in the back of my father's car. Maribel and I never forget that time when I told him that the fun I'd had with my friends during a carefree August could never compensate for the pain I'd felt at losing a match against a player I should have beaten. The pain came from the knowledge that I had given less than my best, that if I'd trained instead of played that August, I would have won my match. That was the day I defined my priorities and, without quite realizing it at the time, made my life's big choice. Having made it, there could be no going back. Not then, not now. The path was set, and while there have been moments of doubt and weakness, I have never deviated from it. Not even when temptation was strongest.

One such moment came on a vacation I went on to Thailand with a group of childhood friends from Manacor. It was a chance to make up for lost time, but my competitive nature rebelled.

A tournament was coming up in Bangkok, and before heading there I decided to take a week off on a beach. There were ten of us, including my oldest friend, Miguel Ángel Munar, with whom I'd trained under Toni as a small boy. As we prepared to leave home, I had my doubts about the benefits of going all the way to Bangkok, fighting jet lag to compete in a tournament that was not especially high in my list of priorities to win. But I had made a commitment to take part eight months earlier and I could not, at this late hour, let the organizers down.

We had a great time on our vacation. We went Jet Skiing and played golf. But I remember what struck Miguel Ángel, who had never spent night and day with me in the week prior to a tournament before, was that no sooner had we landed, after a trip that had included three flight changes, than I headed straight to a tennis court in the hotel complex for an hour's training. He was even more taken aback to discover that, even if we had gone to bed at five in the morning, I'd be up punctually every morning at nine to train—and again for another hour every afternoon.

What Miguel Ángel didn't know was that, fine a time as we were all having, something was bothering me. I was putting in the hours, but I wasn't training as thoroughly as I knew I ought to with a tournament around the corner. We were in the deepest tropics, and the weather was too hot and humid to allow me to exert myself the way I needed to. So I took a decision that did not particularly please my friends, nor did it particularly please me. But it had to be taken. We were scheduled to head back to Bangkok on a Tuesday evening, but I left on the Monday morning. This was not going to be the most important tournament of my career, but having decided to take part, I was not going to give it anything less than my best. If I had kept to the original schedule, I'd have missed out on two days of proper preparation. And that was something I felt I could not afford to do. As it was, I lost in the semifinals, knowing that if I'd had less fun on the beach, on court I would have had more joy.

One lesson I've learned is that if the job I do were easy, I wouldn't derive so much satisfaction from it. The thrill of winning is in direct proportion to the effort I put in before. I also know, from long experience, that if you make an effort in training when you don't especially feel like making it, the payoff is that you will win games when you are not feeling your best. That is how you win championships, that is what separates the great player from the merely good player. The difference lies in how well you've prepared.

Novak Djokovic is one of the contemporary greats, no doubt about it, but, with darkness falling in New York, I was beating him two sets to one. It was nine fifteen when he served at the start of the fourth set. He was playing well, but I was playing very well. I knew he had to be feeling under a lot of strain, having been obliged to play from behind right from the start, at no point finding himself in the lead in the match. And now he was falling further behind. If I went ahead in this set, it was going to be very hard for him mentally. The pressure was on me too, but I had sufficient experience of Grand Slam finals to be confident my game would hold up.

In the very first point of the set I got a lucky break. He delivered a good first serve, putting me on the defensive immediately, then we exchanged a couple of shots and he rushed the net. I tried a cross-court cut on the backhand, but I struck the ball badly, and it turned into an accidental lob. He thought of going for the smash but left it, thinking it was sailing out, but he misjudged the back-spin and the ball dropped just inside the baseline. It was a good point to win but, more than that, a telling reflection of Djokovic's state of mind. He had confirmed my impression that his confidence was fading and he was running out of ideas. Otherwise, he might have hit the smash, and in any case, he would not have been in such a hurry to try and finish the rally quickly by going to the net, something he does as rarely as I do. He was taking more and more risks, and my intuition told me that if I continued to plug away as I was, I'd push him to the edge of despondency.

He won the next point after again rushing the net, this time with a finely angled, cut volley. I sprinted like hell, diagonally the whole length of the court, and almost got to it. It was good he saw me try; that would make him think twice the next time he tried a volley. It might force him to try too hard and make a mistake. At 15–15 we sparred from the baselines for a good while, until he lost his composure and made an unwise attempt to hit a forehand winner, and it went wide. He won the next one after I hit the ball long, but then, after he missed another forehand, I had break point, 30–40. For the first time in the match he let out a loud curse. Maybe he needed to do that; maybe it did him good. But for me it was another encouraging sign.

My main problem right now was that one very important weapon, his serve, was continuing to work well. He had not missed one since the start of the game. And he didn't miss his next three either. He went 1–0 up, but I still had the feeling that he did not have too many bullets left.

Serving well and playing well, I leveled the score on the next game. He won one point, ripping a forehand down the line about as hard as any human being can, but he lost the other four, one to a backhand that he struck well wide, after which he emitted another of those encouraging howls of pain. Then I finished him off with two big serves.

At 1–1, on his serve, I smelled blood. The momentum had been with me since the beginning of the third set, and I was not going to let it go. My legs were fresh and I felt a surge of confidence. He, on the other hand, was tiring in both mind and body, and it showed in the first two points of the game, which he lost badly, with the lamest of shots. His first serve kept working, throwing him a lifeline, but after I ripped a forehand winner past his defenses, he surrendered the game at thirty. I had my break and I served to go 3–1 up.

My tendency when I am ahead is to play defensively, but it was a measure of how well I felt that as the set progressed I was going more and more on the attack, seizing the initiative in one point after another. That was what I did in the first point of the fourth game, moving Djokovic right and left and right again, pounding him, until he had no strength left but to hit a forehand weakly into the net. I won the game at love, two aces included. Having consolidated my break of Djokovic's serve by holding my own, I felt—at 3–1—in command of the match.

An unspoken rule of tennis is that if you are tired you try not to show it. He'd given up trying. His body language reflected resignation, as if he had run out of answers to my challenges. Now was the moment to go for the double break and clinch the match. My instinct again was to play it safe, but my judgment told me the time was ripe for aggression. I didn't want to let up the pressure on Djokovic for one second. I knew how mercurial he was, and the one thing I had to avoid at all costs was giving him a window of opportunity to recover his self-belief and rediscover his best form. I glanced up at my corner, where my team and family were sitting, and saw Tuts smiling broadly, Toni looking as serious and concentrated as usual. I caught his eye, and he muttered to me, so I could just hear above the din, that the moment had come to really go for it. I wanted to hear that. My sternest judge was confirming my own perception of the way the match was going.

I didn't have to push myself as hard as I'd expected to break Djokovic's serve a second time. He flailed at a forehand on the first point, hitting it long, and I hammered home the advantage by winning the next one with a forehand drive that caught him way out of position. Then he double faulted to go 0–40 down. I missed my first chance, looping a forehand long, but then he as much as surrendered the match, yelling in despair after he mishit a simple forehand into the net. I was winning 4–1, two sets to one up and about to serve.

When you are serving as well as I was, you eliminate a whole dimension of anxiety from your game. You're not thinking, as you shape up to serve at the start of a game, "Please, please don't let me down." The rhythm of your serve becomes automated, and your body does its job almost on its own. Mentally, this is of incredible value. You feel a lot calmer, freed up to concentrate on the other aspects of your game.

This was the theory, and should have been so in practice. But no. Because at this point my mind began to play its strange tricks. There I was, about to serve to go 5–1 up, with my opponent clearly on his last legs, and yet I became suddenly possessed by fear, just as at that critical moment in the fourth set at Wimbledon two years earlier. As then, it was the fear of winning that got to me. Every last bit of logic pointed to me having the match wrapped up. How many times in my career had I lost in these circumstances after going a double break ahead? Four, maybe? No, more likely two. Clearly, short of some utterly unexpected catastrophe, the set and the match had to be mine.

But following this train of thought was not, at this stage, the right thing to do. I tried to push away the thoughts of victory that flooded my mind; tried to do what I knew was right, which was to think only of the next point, in isolation from everything else. But I could not, entirely, and as I lined up to deliver my first serve of the game, I felt, quite simply, afraid.

The effect on my serve was immediate. Having worked like clockwork until now, it suddenly started to jam up. My confidence in my ground strokes collapsed, and my movement was all wrong. I started playing much more defensively, and I was scrambling thoughtlessly around the court. My body tensed up, my arm tightened. The knowledge that if I won this game I'd be 5–1 up and the US Open would be practically mine was not useful. The enormity of what I was on the brink of achieving now made me feel as if I were face-to-face with a giant monster about to swallow me up. And I froze. Or almost froze.

I did get the first serve of the first point in. It was a percentage serve, safe, no sting in it, but enough to get the rally going, banishing the risk of a double fault, which was an achievement in itself. Luckily, Djokovic's morale was shot, and the rally ended with him hitting the ball needlessly wide. Then I lost the next point going for a forehand winner down the line. I had been holding my service games comfortably all set until now. This one was torture. We got to deuce. We got back to deuce twice more. I saved one break point. Then he suddenly conjured a couple of devastating winners. But he was being erratic: for each thunderous drive, an unforced error. I was still holding the line, not making any unforced errors.

On the third deuce, he rushed to the net behind a powerful fore-hand to my backhand corner. I almost had to kneel to dig it out, but I managed to get all the strength of my arms behind the ball and whipped it cross-court for a winner. Somehow, instinct had kicked in, beating the nerves, and I had pulled off one of my best shots of the match.

My serve was too much for him on the next point. He hit the return long and it was over. I was 5–1 up.

The tension washed off. He was serving now, and I was not ex-pecting to win this game. I was expecting to win the next one. I had a sensation of calm after the storm, and yes, I played the game as if I were half-asleep. I am not proud of that. He won the game at thirty with an angled drop volley that I didn't even try to run for.

Serving for the match at 5–2, the nerves returned. They are al-ways there. As difficult to conquer as your opponent across the net, and, like your opponent, sometimes they are up, sometimes they are down. Right now they were the biggest remaining obstacle between me and victory. I looked up at my corner, saw the old familiar faces, elated, shouting encouragement. Inside I wanted so much to win this for them, for all of us, but my face—a good face—betrayed nothing.

The nerves were getting to everybody. Djokovic hit his return of serve long on the first point, and then the line judge declared one of his balls out that had clearly hit the line. We had to replay the point. Everything was life-and-death now, and this changed call was a blow. I had to put it out of my mind immediately and keep reminding myself to play steadily, nothing clever, give him plenty of room to make mistakes.

On the second point he went for another drop. This time I did run for it, and made it. He reached the volley, and I, my nose almost touching the net, volleyed the ball right back to win the point, 30–0.

The crowd, unable to stay quiet during this point, as in many previous points, went nuts—Toni more so than anyone. I looked up and saw him over to my left. He was on his feet, fists clenched, trying not to cry. I did cry. With the towel I wiped the tears away from my eyes. Through the blur, I saw it; I saw victory now. I knew I shouldn't, but I did.

Not quite yet, though. He got a lucky net cord on the next point, and the ball dribbled over my side of the net. Inwardly, I cursed. I could have been 40–0 up and in a position to play the next point calmly, knowing it was all over. Instead, more stress. And then he made it to thirty all after I hurried my shot too much, missing an attempt at a forehand winner. My heart was racing, nerves battling with elation. Just two more points and I'd make it. I tried hard to stay focused, saying to myself, "Play easy, no risks, just keep the ball in."

This time I followed my script. The rally was a long one, fifteen shots. We exchanged a dozen hard baseline punches, and then he came to the net behind a deep drive to my backhand corner. This time it was me who got a touch of luck. The ball skimmed the top of the net, and as he managed to stab it back over, I ran diagonally across the court and scooped up the forehand. He was expecting me to hit cross-court. Instead, I went down the line, and the ball, heavy with topspin, looped in. Just. Djokovic couldn't believe it. He issued a challenge; he was wrong. The screen showed the ball had gone in, by a millimeter, brushing the outside of the baseline. Djokovic crouched down and bowed his head, the image of defeat. Toni, Titín, and my father clenched their fists, screaming *"Vamos!"* Tuts, my mother, and my sister applauded, laughing with joy. María Francisca had her hands on her head, as if not believing what seemed to be about to happen.

Match point. Championship point. Everything point. I glanced up at my team, as if imploring them to give me courage, seeking from them some measure of calm. Fighting back tears again, I served. Wide to the backhand, as instructed. The rally lasted six shots. On the sixth he hit the ball wide, well wide, and out. My legs buckled and I fell to the ground before the ball had even landed, and I stayed there, facedown, sobbing, my body shaking.

Collapsing to the ground like that is not something you plan. I didn't realize I was doing it. My mind stopped, raw emotion took over, and as the tension broke, so did my body, unable to bear its weight anymore. All of a sudden, as if recovering consciousness after blacking out, I realized I was stretched out on the court, under a cascade of noise, and I saw what I had accomplished. At the age of twenty-four I'd won four Grand Slams; I'd made history, I'd achieved something greater than anything I had ever dared dream of, something that would last all my life and no one would ever take away from me. Whatever happened next, I'd leave the game of tennis one day as someone who'd been important in the sport, as one of the best, and hopefully—for I thought this too at my moment of triumph—as someone who people considered to be a good person.

Novak Djokovic—or "Nole," as I call him, as do his fans, friends, and family—is all of these things already. Extraordinarily gracious at a moment so bitter for him, he didn't wait for me at the net but came over to my side of the court and embraced me, congratulated me on what I had done. I went to my chair, dropped off my racket, and came back to the center of the ring with my fists in the air. The noise of the crowd poured down on me, and I sank to my knees, sobbed again, bowed my forehead onto the hard surface of the court, and held it there. So, so much had gone into this and I had so, so much to be grateful for.

In the presentation ceremony Nole was the first to speak, and once again, he behaved with great class, showering praise on me and thanking absent friends. He showed himself to be the most dignified of losers and a credit to our sport. When my turn came to address the microphone, I thanked all the members of my family and my team gathered there before me, and reminded them of my life's biggest truth: I could not have done it without them. I made a special mention of Joan Forcades, who was watching back home. Yes, Joan was right. The sum is greater than the parts, and the biggest part of all is the people around me. But I'd felt exceptionally fit and strong during the US Open, and that had given me an edge that day over Nole, and Joan had had a big part to play in that. I also made a point of acknowledging Nole's attitude in defeat, and what a great example he set to kids everywhere. I said I was sure he'd be winning this trophy very soon, as I am sure he will continue to be a fearsome rival in the years to come. But this was my moment. For all the passion and work I had invested for so long in trying to make myself as good a tennis player as I could be, this was truly something I had never imagined. As I held up the US Open trophy and the cameras flashed and the crowd roared, I understood that I had made the impossible possible. I was, for that brief moment, on top of the world.

MANACOR

THE ROUND OF MEDIA interviews after the US Open final lasted three hours, almost as long as the match itself. Nadal patiently answered each question, the most recurrent of which was "What can you do to match that?" The answer, always the same, was "Work hard, try and be a better player, and be back here next year."

At one in the morning he left for dinner with his family and his team at a restaurant in Manhattan, not to emerge until after three. At nine he was doing a street-side interview with NBC's *Today Show*, and from there, pursued by a swelling mob of fans, he did as New York protocol required and posed for photographs in Times Square. Car horns blared, and a phalanx of police held back the screaming crowds. Then it was off to a couple of live TV studio interviews and after that an event with Nike hosted by one of his biggest fans, the charismatic former American tennis champion John McEnroe. Nadal swam in a sea of adulation. All the talk was of his records: the first player to win consecutive Grand Slam titles on clay, grass, and hard courts in a calendar year; the seventh player in history to win four Grand Slams, the youngest to do so, at twenty-four, in the Open era.

He made it just in time to JFK Airport for his flight home that evening, arriving in Manacor the next day, at noon. There were no brass bands, there was no welcoming committee, no fuss at all. That night he went out on the town with his childhood friends and next morning, at 5 A.M. New York time, he was back on court, hitting balls with his uncle Toni, both of them rapt and serious as ever, as if there was still everything to play for and little had been achieved.

The municipal sports center where they trained was practically empty. In the parking lot Nadal's sports car stood out alongside three other vehicles; on the running track was a solitary sprinter; of the dozen hard courts, only one other was in use. No locals had thought it worth their while to come and watch, much less pay homage to the biggest global celebrity their town was ever likely to produce, the man regarded by many at that particular moment as the greatest athlete alive. Only two onlookers were there, an elderly German couple who took photographs silently, from a safe distance, having correctly sensed that the ceremony between nephew and uncle was taking place on forbidden territory. Nadal's father, Sebastián, made an appearance later, but he knew not to interrupt his son and his brother who, in a telepathic trance inside their closed world, did not cast him a glance.

On a court alongside them two middle-aged men in shorts were locked in battle, scrambling around, as club players do, in ungainly pursuit of gently looping balls, paying no attention whatsoever to the supreme exponent of the game displaying his rhythmic repertoire on the other side of the fence netting. They were not impressed, or if they were, they were not going to show it. Just the way Nadal's family has always treated him; just the way he likes it when he is back home in Manacor.

CAREER HIGHLIGHTS

1994

Under-12 champion of the Balearic Islands, age 8

1997

Under-12 national champion of Spain

2000

Under-14 national champion of Spain

2002

First victory in the Association of Tennis Professionals circuit,
  age 15

2004

Won the Davis Cup, representing Spain, age 18

2005

French Open champion: first Grand Slam title, age 19

2006

French Open champion

2007

French Open champion

2008

French Open champion

Wimbledon champion

Number one in the world rankings

Gold Medal, Beijing Olympics

2009

Australian Open champion

2010

French Open champion

Wimbledon champion

US Open champion, completed Career Grand Slam

2011

French Open champion: Tenth Grand Slam title, age 25